Through the Windows of God

SHARI KA

TRAFFORD
PUBLISHING™

Order this book online at www.trafford.com
or email orders@trafford.com

Most Trafford titles are also available at major online book retailers.

Printed in the United States of America.

ISBN: 978-1-4669-5534-9 (sc)
ISBN: 978-1-4669-5535-6 (e)

Library of Congress Control Number: 2012916009

Trafford rev. 09/20/2012

 www.trafford.com

North America & international
toll-free: 1 888 232 4444 (USA & Canada)
phone: 250 383 6864 ♦ fax: 812 355 4082

I wish to thank Dr. David Kesteman for the cover photos. David took these amazing photos while visiting Jamaica. I love the photos and they are perfect for this book!

I wish to thank my loving friends and family for encouraging me to write and to continue to write these messages, I believe God has given me to share with all those who read and share these thoughts. God has blessed me with many gifts and this passion for using His words to express something good to help another along their journey in this life has brought blessings of peacefulness to my heart and soul. I have learned much from this journey.

If anything I have written has touched another's life in a positive way and helped make one's path through this life easier, then I have accomplished my purpose for writing this book. Even if it is just one... only God knows.

May our Loving God be with each of you in all things great and small... remember, there is nothing more valuable and powerful to all humanity, than sincere, heart-felt prayer where-ever there is need. God truly loves... you...

Contents

Through The Windows of God . . . I define me

I, a single, solitary being, moving with awe-struck curiosity along my journey's path of uncertainty . . . this path I must ultimately walk alone, for this is each one's reality. Each one must stand alone before God. Not one thing, not one place, not one person great can change this, for we are absolute and singular before our God. Each one is defined through the all knowing windows of God . . . there an open awareness of His majestic power . . . there through His wisdom loaned . . . I define me. Alone standing before the windows of God, I search for all of tomorrow's, hopes and destinies . . . visions of my own honesty beckons me to come hither, to open spaces beyond imagination's celestial doors, I bow to heaven's promises and there . . . Truth defines me.

In this stillness of solidarity, this place I go to contemplate, to contemplate God and me, to contemplate the molding of me and who I am supposed to be. In this silent place He waits for me, bathed in His infinite, all consuming power 'tis His light of love, this love His offerings to me. In this silence I call out to me and He. I seek answers to tests complete and tests, yet to be won. This, a time I ask of His mystery's revelations and His loving purposes for me. He breathed my name . . . behold, then came the proclamation of my future's destiny. His miracle became me . . . through the windows of God; I stand before a reflection of me from He.

How do I thank Thee, how do I give thanks to One who breathed life into this existence and I, He lovingly entrusted in Angel's hands came to be, I became me. I wish to thank Thee through wisdom's gifts He has given me. I work to be all He has hoped that I will be, I work with wisdom's absolute sincerity. This path I walk with heart of humbled gratitude, gratitude for lending my hungry soul the light of His Heavenly Spirit's mastery . . . He that breathed and I became me, this miracle of life He gifted is me.

How do I define me? Do I look to troubles unfair, do I praise all efforts I have won, do I caress to my heart's purest places the cruelness of the world's citizens forlorn, truly bent on crushing the hopes of this miracle God gave to me . . . this miracle that is me? Do I compare my lesser endowments to those blessed differently than me? Yes, this is how I define me, yes I learn from all that has touched me and take the good of it, only the good I allow is the defining of me. The cruelness I hear not, for that is not about me. I am better when I am delivered up to this one's unrelenting agony, for I pray for this troubled one's rescue. I ask God for mercies and deliverance from this one's prison of cruelty. I pray for forgiveness only God can bestow, to heal this one's heart so burdened and low, then blessings I win to the betterment of me, now greater is beauty's definition of me.

Through the windows of God . . . I define me, for I am born a part of He as He breathed His breath into me. This once lifeless form of dust, then became the living soul of me. Each time I look into the windows of God, there I see . . . I see His reflection looking back at me . . . His reflection feeding all needs be . . . this is the me I wish for you to see . . . rewards of His reflection looking back at me, for there you will ever see me . . . through the windows of God.

A Farmer's Prayer

Yonder glows the morning sun,
As the world in silent slumber sleeps.
'tis toil to get a days work done,
His work awaits and will not keep.

He gazes past the ground below,
He looks beyond what surface shows.
A prayerful glance to the sky,
A heart filled with pleading hope.

His life he gives to tend the soil,
His heart, his sweat and anguish bear.
His tears, his time, his promise made,
As life goes on, so unaware.

Each new day he knows the truth,
In every seed he sees God's hand.
Awe 'n wonder awaken his soul,
He sees His work in all the land.

Yonder glows the morning sun,
The world in silent slumber sleeps.
A farmer's prayer lifts up at dawn,
His work awaits and will not keep.

A Farmer's Prayer . . . was inspired by a dear friend of mine. He was an elderly, very interesting and intelligent man. He was an Attorney, retired from his private practice. He became a Real Estate Attorney for a major Southern Indiana college, which is where I met him, while I was attending classes there and we became golfing buddies. He was an excellent golfer and we enjoyed many afternoons hitting the ball around several different courses all over southern Indiana.

Will was interested in my writing and enjoyed sharing his thoughts about a new topic that I had written. Will asked me to write a poem about farmers. He went on to tell me, in his opinion, farmers are a much ignored profession and that society rarely gives farmers and what they do much thought. Farmers are taken for granted, according to Will and I think in many ways, I agree with Will. Think about it, what would we do with-out our farmers?

I sat down and with-in a few minutes at my key board, A Farmer's Prayer came to be. To this day, it is one of my favorite poems. Will loved the poem and I dedicate this poem to Will and all of the hard working farmers out there. Thank you for all you do! I appreciate you!

If I were a Butterfly

. . . what would I feel . . .
I would fly all around
with such grace and zeal.

I would find each flower,
I'd choose one by one,
not caring the color,
'tis nectar, taste 'n fun.

If I were a butterfly
what would I feel . . .
the damp morning dew,
the afternoon sun.

I'd dance through the air
'til darkness come.
I'd hide 'n folded wings
when day is done.

If I were a butterfly
. . . what would I feel . . .
as I dip and soar,
I'd fly so high
'til I was no more!!

If I Were a Butterfly . . . this poem seems to be a favorite with most people. The inspiration for this poem came to me while I was watching a lone butterfly, busily flying from flower to flower, then flying high in the sky, just to come down again to another flower. I sat down at my key board, thinking about this butterfly and this poem came to be . . .

Time's Whisper

My time has passed for earth's good joy, for earth's great toil and lessons . . . now finally done. I tried and failed and tried and gained, the best and worst of all life's challenges, to pass my journey's course. I faced and fought distain while embracing my life's work, a work most times well done.

My time on earth so quickly spent, I with youthful eyes did not see, for many days what was becoming so evident. My body worn and tired by time's unrelenting call, I turned to see me, yet this reflection looking back is one of frailty . . . this frailty is a gift time has made of me. Yes, it is a gift time has given me. In this face, time's messages I see.

Grieve not for me, for we knew some day this would be my welcoming destiny. I did not want to leave you, for I know your heart will be heavy and sad. Oh, but I, so wanted to go where God's promised hope is my reality. Weariness has spoken to my spirit's fading will . . . weariness has readied me . . .

My time has passed for earth's good joy, for earth's great toil and lessons . . . now finally done . . . Time's whisper has been longingly beckoning me, Time's whisper has now proclaimed the all of me . . . I am forever your precious memory.

Time's Whisper . . . This grievance poem is inspired by those that are ready to pass on, yet have concerns about leaving loved ones behind or causing their loved ones pain . . . I have written several grievance poems, to speak to those who are grieving the loss of a loved one. Each grievance poem was inspired by the hurting and loss of the living. I think many folks just need to know that their loved one is safe and with God and really are in a better place.

Thoughts of my own mother and her passing helped inspire this writing. She was ready to be with God and in her special, most loving way, told us all good-bye, then quietly, peacefully slipped away.

Ann

Ann, each whispering note caresses my imagination's visions, then carries me to where all innocence is awakened from beneath the rubble of now and yesterday's callings. I drift hypnotically away, as you touch each note, while possessing all good, which is sleeping within me . . . this yearning sleeps, patiently inside me. With each gentle stroke of your piano keys, Ann, Angels joyfully dance, as your fingers glide each key, whispering an undeniable beckoning to the deepest part of me. Ann, you awaken my day-dream's smoldering tranquility, as though your Angels choreographed each chord with echoes of Heaven's exhilaration, such awe and fervor only expressed by the passion of you . . . only by the passion of your gift, Ann.

Ann, each whispering note caresses imagination's visions, then carries me to where all innocence is awakened, as my enlightened spirit surrenders, each chord manifests visions of a wilderness song, bath in unsung wonder . . . there . . . engaged in anticipations hidden places of my soul, your magical notes and chords claim the very essence of me. Ann, this . . . as each key answers to the passion of your methodical touch . . . a proclamation that only God can orchestrate, this impassioned gift . . . this infinite, burning brilliance from the soul of you . . . this defining flow of Heaven's inspiration, so wondrously exudes only from the soul of you . . . only from the soul of you, Ann.

Ann, A Place in the Sun . . . Ann is an amazing pianist!! If I am having a not so good day, I can listen to her music and it brings me back into balance. I honestly get lost in her music. I was listening to her music, as I wrote this writing titled, Ann. I am so impressed, as to how she plays the piano with such gracefulness and a heavenly sound.

When I listen to Ann's music on a day that is a good day for me, the sounds of her piano make it a great day. Ann has an exceptional and amazing gift, surely from the very heart of God.

As The Butterflies Dance

I wind the road, through trees and hills. A heavy heart with saddened will. No light to feel, to see, no light of day to brighten the darkness of me . . . , then magic, as magic will, that moment my world stood still, as I turn the last bend I see, a wonderment awaiting me, a wonderment to erase all cares, a heavenly sight awaiting there.

My soul felt joy with the welcoming sight of the butterflies dancing in luminous sunlight. Flowers reaching to sunlight's call, embracing each butterfly, as they glide by. Surely Angels and rainbows orchestrated this colorful gift. I stand in awe at this sight, the butterflies skip and sour to nature's harmony, this greeting I know was meant just for me. A loveliness that only God could make, ah, a butterfly dance, just for my sake.

Butterflies moving with silent grace to compositions of Angel's songs. I stand in awe, as my soul can hear beyond the silence, the cords and notes, as the butterflies dance. Each note an awareness comes to say, I have been away too long. With each breath of wind, the butterflies glide in performance surely Angels guide. The butterflies dance a language of softened strength, spoken with each dip and sour, a message I will always hold dear, I have been away too long, I have been away too long, this I hear, I feel and know, as the butterflies dance a welcome for me . . . , I have been away too long, too long . . . in awe is my stance . . . as the butterflies dance.

As The Butterflies Dance . . . this was inspired by what I am sharing with you in this writing. I had been away from home for quite some time and during that time, I had a heart rendering event happen. My drive-way was ¼ mile long and wound through the woods. My heart was feeling very heavy, as I drove up the drive, through the woods to my home. As I rounded the last bend and stopped my car in front of my house, this writing describes exactly what I saw and felt, as I watched the butterflies. I felt the most incredible calm come over me, as I watched at least 30 butterflies, flying, so gracefully all about the butterfly bushes. I got out of my car and stood for the longest time, watching the butterflies dance all about the blossoms. I stood there in a spell-bound awe of this sight. God is so kind to provide us with just what we need when we need Him most. This is the gift that He gave to me that day.

Forgive Yourself

To forgive yourself allows you to grow and be open to realize God's peace. Perfection is not a quality that we will ever master, therefore one must expect and accept that we will, at times be at fault. God's forgiveness allows one the freedom to grow beyond our faults.

Think on this, if you will not forgive self for the wrongs of yesterday, then are you not frozen in that negative vault of time? There can be no other conclusion, but that you are. Ask yourself, is this a place that can bring wisdom, joy and peace? God's will is that you not be cemented in time by your feelings of guilt. There can be no positive growth in a place of torment. God created you to be happy.

God offers, by grace, a safe route for all things in your life. To forgive your self can be a release from the bondage of guilt. You cannot be open to God's truths and grow with wisdom if you are blocked by your self made walls of shame. Think on this . . . can you grow if you carry the weight of guilt? To hold onto the wrongs of yesterday is to diminish your opportunity for a peaceful tomorrow.

The forgiveness that I speak of is from God. He is waiting with love and wants to take away your bonds. He is waiting to set your heart free. The given ability to forgive your self is a gift of love from God. With a heart that is free, God's love can grow within you. You can see and experience the beauty of life when burdens are lifted. You can know God and His ever-growing peace if you will give God the wrongs of yesterday and have faith that you are free . . . Follow His ensample . . . set yourself free, then go in peace and be.

Forgive Yourself . . . this writing was inspired by knowing folks that have made mistakes, as well, as myself and being unable to move on from whatever the event was/is. This writing is a message to all of us . . . we are to learn from and let go of our mistakes. Folks seem to isolate themselves, as if they are the only person to ever make mistakes or the kind of mistakes they may have made. This is not so, we are all guilty from time to time, this is a part of our journey and learning experiences. It is wrong to never let go of your wrongs and to keep beating yourself up. If we can't forgive ourselves and go on, then we can never have a full and peaceful life of learning.

Gina

She walks in a silence only Angels know. Gentle breezes whisper a welcome, as her delicate, silhouette, quietly commands the radiance of her garden flowers just by her presence.

Ah, she comes to tend to her beloved blossoms with an eager heart of care. She bends to touch each one, not for another course, but to let each one know she is there. Her essence is, as a breath of life, as she graces the midst of a solitary moment. Her pause is, but a message of all answers to her garden's place. With a sense of her, each flower gently sways in wait.

Even butterflies dance, as she purposely goes about with labor of love. Tending to the flowers, she understands the very birth of each magnificent blossom is a gift, a first birth sent from above.

Her soul feels a mirror reflection of self at peace, as she skillfully, lovingly nurtures her flowers in her garden place and need. As the world turns in trouble and with unsettled unrest . . . she shares only a loveliness, a place where flowers grow, the boundaries of her garden where only love is manifest.

As day light dims and the sun slowly fades behind a distant hill, she turns to leave her garden, yet relentlessly she goes . . . with pleading thoughts of time's impatience. Her presence will ever grace this garden, for her essence is etched in moment's collected eternity. Her spirit touching this moment in time . . . her place in her garden will always be . . . as she walks in a silence only Angles know . . . her place nary dim . . . as Gina walks with silent footsteps, where only Garden Angels surely go.

Gina . . . this is inspired by Gina. Gina is a beautiful person. So intelligent, so full of life and she loved flower gardening and she was very good at it. Gina and I worked together and our working relationship was a very good one. I loved to watch Gina make flower baskets for people, because it seemed she had a gift that none other shared.

Gina was funny, interesting and very talented with whatever she set her mind to do. Gina was loved and respected by many. Gina was very well known for her work in the Arts Dept. at a major southern Indiana College. She held a Master's degree from that same college, as well, as many other accomplishments.

Gina became very ill. I wrote this writing about Gina when I learned of her illness. Not long after I wrote this, she passed away. The loss was great for all that knew Gina. That was a very sad day.

At her memorial service, this poem, Gina was read . . . to this day, I feel honored that Gina's family chose to share this poem, my vision of Gina. I think that all who really knew her, had this same vision of this uniquely, special lady . . . Gina.

Gossips

Gossips are thieves of truth, peace and unity. Their joy is to steal the best of thee . . . to weaken society's woven bonds of harmony.

They come by the night of darkened hearts, to whisper untruth's words to all who draw near. Words to condemn, words to separate, words of judgments untold, words of delight to all gossip's ears . . . words they eagerly behold.

They sing words of folly, as in Summer's delight, yet winter's chill of darkness owns the gossips heart. They go to and fro, serving only a victim's grief . . . to all mankind, they are . . . , but a filthy thief.

An eager audience is ever near, they add this or take away that, "oh it must be true", they say, "it must be true, for all my words are truths, a burdening message I need to bear."

The gossip's task is never done, seeking to destroy the best of any one. A gossip hides in pretense's vanity, a place of courage's vacancy. A darkened place hidden while boasting self, proclaimed honesty, yet a place never hidden from God, the victim's mastery.

A gossip's words are recorded, each one by one . . . , the God of mercy leaves not untruth's rewards undone. The victim's tears are counted too . . . , by Angel's hands, as they catch the pain of weeping dew.

A message of comfort untold, a message for a broken victim to behold. God's Son a spotless man, a victim held in the gossip's hands. When gossip's words rein ore all a victim's joy . . . , one thought will sustain 'til God's will proclaims . . . , look what they did to Jesus Christ . . . , compassion's absolute truth . . . He, the gossip's victim too . . . , just the same as me and you.

Gossips . . . this was inspired by the gossip that I worked with that also inspired the writing, "What They Say." I listened to this person gossip about folks nearly every day. Sometimes she would be in a conversation with another that also participated in her gossip, which I found appalling. This writing was inspired by this cruelty . . .

Remember . . . if you believe gossip about one you do not know, or judge another's true circumstance, then what does that say about you?

. . . walk a mile in my shoes . . .

Grace

Grace, a white haired beauty with a name God pondered, as He looked ahead in time. A name surely God and Angels, through Heaven's harmony gave. A name that speaks of absolute love, tenderness and compassion . . . a name bestowing God's own heart and namesake . . . there . . . is Grace.

Grace, she bears the face of God's peaceful Spirit, with expressions of wisdom's special knowing and nurturing gifts . . . there . . . is Grace, with her Angelic glow.

As Grace sits quietly at family gatherings, all eyes are drawn to her loveliness, for there is none on this earthly journey to compare. Her soft white hair crowns her presence, as that of an Angelic halo.

As a part of God's master plan, our souls are ever drawn to the light . . . and there . . . sitting quietly with salvation's gentleness, caressing her sweet face . . . there . . . is Grace . . . a white haired beauty with a name surely God and Angels knew to give . . . Grace, she . . . a reminder of God's presence and love. His love ever there, each time our eyes gaze upon the face of such warmth and loveliness . . . this . . . the face of Grace.

Grace . . . this writing was inspired by Grace. She is the most lovely, Angelic woman, with a delicate face, framed with the whitest hair. She truly is beautiful. She is in her 90's, so fragile and tiny, yet there is a glow about this sweet lady that draws your attention.

Grace is usually at family gatherings, sitting quietly, smiling, so sweetly at everyone. She seems to truly love everyone in her presence, because she always greets all others with genuine kindness.

Grace brings special warmth to all those fortunate enough to gaze upon the Angelic face of, Grace.

Just a Thought Away

When the winds softly caress your face and lift your thoughts to other places of yesterday, I am there. The memory of me is me. I am ever with you, for I am . . . just a thought away.

All I am is still, as I took the Angel's hand . . . I changed to God's perfection, but did not cease, I am still the me of me. Look up high and call my name, in the light of you, I remain. Tears run down your face, as you search in anguish the echoes of me in your agony. Desperation's tears fall with helpless groans, as your soul is bent beneath the utterance of your crying . . . Oh, I am reaching out in your visions of me, it is me, I am with you . . . , for I am just a thought away.

When the cold winds blow and the skies are grey, lift your thoughts to me, for I am the warmth you seek, comforting your soul with loving memories. When violets grace the lane and each one nods to breezes unassuming directions . . . I am just a thought away.

Look for me in all of our familiar places, for there is where you will find me. Close your eyes and allow your visions to call to me, for I did not leave you, I am there. Your thoughts of me are a beckoning I will ever answer . . . , for I am just a thought away.

Turn to the sense of something familiar, turn and search the alls of me, the alls of our memories. I am still me, I did not cease, for love never dies. Our history has etched an eternal essence of our love in the safety of your heart. It is me, it is us . . . you and I will ever be. The memory of me is me, the memory of me is me. Set your heart's visions free . . . then you will see, you will sense, you will hear, you will know . . . the memory of me is me . . . for I will always be . . . just a thought away.

Just a Thought Away . . . was inspired by a married couple that I knew. This couple was unusually close, as they seldom went anywhere without the other. Their lives were intertwined in most all things. They were married for many years, raised a family and remained living in the same little house where they raised their children. William retired and he and Joyce planned to travel, which they had been doing since William's retirement.

One evening, William was feeling very ill. He became so ill, Joyce took him to the local Emergency Room. William was only there a short time when he passed away from a massive heart attack.

The grief that Joyce experienced touched me, so deeply that I sat down and wrote this poem. I believe every word in this poem is true and I think it was meant just for Joyce from her loving William.

As I sat down to write this, the words came so easily, as though William was speaking to Joyce and I think he was. I sent this poem to Joyce and it meant so much to her and it was comforting for her to realize that William is, just a thought away.

Lewisport

I wander down your streets in awe,
With visions of life before. Old buildings
Standing, some straight and tall,
Some lazy with age's decline,
As they reckon with the relentlessness of time.

Visions of busy merchants, hard working folks,
Some in horse drawn buggies as they hurried on,
Some sitting on benches,
Outside a neighborhood store.

Oh, each hand that labored and toiled,
Each pair of feet that carried on.
A brick to bake, a board to saw,
Each brow that sweat, each back bent low,
Every groan of agony and shout of joy . . . ,
Is ever etched in the echoes of your eternal walls.

Our dreams carried us to walk your streets,
As our life's journeys continue to unfold . . .
And I, as many before me, will never say good-bye.

Lewisport . . . this is inspired by this sleepy, small town in Kentucky. Lewisport was built on the banks of the beautiful Ohio River. I was so honored to live there for a few years and become acquainted with many of the residents. Many of the people there seem untouched by the outside world's influences. I met so many lovely souls in Lewisport that I will never forget. This poem says just what it is like to walk down the streets of Lewisport. It seems that most of the town has been untouched by time. It is easy for one to walk those streets and allow your thoughts to go back in time, for walking past many of the old, well kept buildings is, as if you step back to when all was new and bustling.

When I moved from that community, I left a piece of my heart there. I go back to refresh my visions of this lovely town. Lewisport will always have a special place in my heart. Again, Thank you George and all of the lovely people I was blessed to have met in Lewisport.

Lucille

Sunday morning and there she is, sitting quietly bent and bowed by history's relentless time. A history that surely Angels help to orchestrate. A history obviously mastered by God's own hand . . . just for Lucille, a history His gift of time He uniquely gave.

She smiles and whispers the softest "hello" and takes my hand. She apologizes, because she cannot stand, but "oh Lucille, although bent low, you stand taller than all, every time your sweet smile touches my soul"

When my time has slowly spent and bends my back by history's whispering call, I want to be just like Lucille . . . sitting in the last pew where surely her Angels lovingly abound and there, my Angels will abide with me too. "Lucille, I want to be like you."

Just peer into those gentle eyes and there you will see a bidding of Angel's songs, every note in heavenly harmony, every note the essence of preciousness . . . God's own loveliness, a loveliness He created just for Lucille . . . this loveliness she shares with you and me. Just peer into those gentle eyes and there you will see . . .

Sunday morning and there she is, sitting quietly in the last pew. Lucille with her essence of preciousness from God, her beauty she is so unaware, her beauty none to compare . . . never to duplicate. Sunday morning and there she is sitting quietly in the last pew. I just know that many times precious Lucille is bent in prayer just for me and you.

Lucille . . . this writing is inspired by Lucille. I attended an old country church, where Lucile's husband is the Pastor. His name is Lawrence and he is the most amazing speaker and one of the most devoted men of God. One can hear his wisdom and love for God every time he speaks and see it in his eyes.

Lucille is so small and frail. She sits in the back, last pew at every service, greeting every one with her soft, almost inaudible greetings. She at times apologizes, because she is unable to stand.

Every time I looked upon Lucille, sitting there with her precious, faint smile, I just felt warm with a special love for this beautiful lady. I wanted to put my visions of Lucille in print, so I sat down at my key board and these thoughts came to me . . . this, the writing of Lucille.

Unconditional Love

When I arrive home from a day at work, he is there to greet me with such excitement and absolute joy. He runs to my arms and I hold him close, letting him know I missed him too. This is our unconditional love.

He stares at me while I'm eating, knowing I can't resist sharing what I have with him, so I bend down, sit beside him and we eat my meal together. Oh, what love I feel, as I hand feed him every bite. This is our unconditional love.

When I am sad or when I cry, he comes to me with his tail down and lays beside me just close enough to touch. He is sad too, for he knows my pain. This is our unconditional love.

Everywhere I go, if at all possible, he goes too. We stop and get him a burger, as he has grown to expect every time we have an outing. I break it up for him at times feeding it to him . . . this, another bonding, mending us to a place I feel we are one. This is our absolute love.

The few times I have had to leave him in the care of another, knowing he was safe and loved . . . he was always in my thoughts and I missed him, knowing how much he was missing me too. This is our unconditional love.

The years slip, so quickly by. Soon time became unkind to his beautiful little body. He cannot seem to rest and nothing I can do seems to help him feel better. He no longer plays and no longer shows the happiness that was once him, he can no longer hear my words of comfort, for he is deaf . . . he can no longer see my smile, for he is blind . . . he can no longer stand, for time has stolen his strength. My heart is truly broken when I see his agonizing struggles. I want to keep him forever. This is our unconditional love.

That day came unexpected. I looked at him, then I, unselfishly understood his pain, anguish and the weariness of his daily struggles. I looked past me and saw only him, then I knew it was time. It was only for him this time, for I knew my pain had just begun. From the day he came into my heart, it was always he and me. It is time to let go and walk the rest of the way without him. With no thoughts of me, it is time to set him free . . . to rest in the arms of Angels . . . this is my unconditional love.

In loving memory of Buffy: February 4, 1989 to March 3, 2005.

Unconditional Love . . . this writing is most special to me. It is inspired by my little Shih Tzu dog, named Buffy. I got Buffy from a breeder when he was 8 weeks old. When I went to pick out a puppy, there were 3 adorable puppies in kennels, stacked one on the other. The first one the owner handed me was hyper, yet so cute. The breeder asked me what personality I wanted and I told him, "I prefer a quiet dog." I looked into the bottom kennel and there was this sweet, little guy laying quietly with his head down and his eyes looking up at me. I asked the owner if I could see that puppy and he took the puppy out and handed him to me. As soon, as I laid him on my shoulder, he snuggled in my hair and fell to sleep. My heart knew, this is the one . . . we bonded the moment I held him. I fell in love with this puppy at that very moment. I believe he knew this, because he was so content in my arms from that day on.

I named him Buffy. He was my constant companion for nearly 17 years. He was the sweetest, most loving little guy. I never imagined my life with-out him. Never imagined it. Buffy became very ill, blind and deaf. He could no longer stand, so I knew it was time to set him free to go back to God. That was the most heart breaking day of my life . . .

Today, I still miss Buffy. I have other dogs, but there will always be, just one Buffy. Buffy and I were a perfect match and probably a once in a life time compatibility. I wrote this writing the day after he passed and my heart still feels just as raw from missing him so . . . Buffy loved me unconditionally, as I do him . . .

What they say . . .

Yonder walks that man, "a man of no good, they say, a man out to do all wrong and guide you astray." I heard he was so unkind to his wife, a man no good to his children too, a man not meant for the company of you.

I heard of his every indiscretion, indiscretions untold, a coldest heart he does behold. They walk the other way . . . too good for this man's company, I heard this as truth, for this is what they say, yes, and if you listen, they will say this to you too.

Yes, . . . I did listen to what they say, yet with soul searching doubt, so I talked with that man today. Ah, he was so kind, not at all as they say . . . cruel, selfish and unkind?! He was so polite, a hand he offered and never a smite.

His smile so sweet and without pretense, his smile of honesty, he never offered a moment to relent. He, of a softer kind. He, so caring and earnestly offering uplifting hopes to this heart of mine. He, never once said a thing about they, he, just smiled and said, they are all o-k.

"Oh, my gosh!!!" "What have they done?! I might have hurt him . . . had I listened to what they say." I am so happy I look to God every day, I listen to Him and not become, as they.

If I listen to everything they say, never getting to know that one for what he is to me . . . not they . . . if I blindly, mindlessly judge another by what they say, then what does that say about me? It surely must say, I am not at all I portray myself to be, for I pride myself on honesty. I walk my path with head held high with proclamations of God's words, not they and I. Is what they say the way God wants me to be?

So . . . if I believe they . . . not what that man has shown to me . . . if I believe they, before I have given that man a chance to share with me . . . if I believe they, before he has even spoken a word to me, if I believe they, knowing God's will for me and he, if I believe they and believe so mindlessly . . . , then . . . what does that say about they and me?

What They Say . . . this was inspired by a co-worker that was a thorn in the side of many, yet face to face, everyone's best friend. Usually I tuned her out. On this particular day, she was berating someone I did not know, as was with many days in her company. Weeks went by and this very person she was berating came to work at our place of employment. After this person was there for awhile, I became acquainted with him and discovered what a kind and caring person he truly is. Surprise!! Nothing she said about him was true.

I wrote this, because so many times others, with-out questioning, believe idle gossip, as if it is truth. This is so wrong!! Never listen to the negative opinions of others. Get to know a person and learn what they are to you, not an idle gossip's negativity.

I believe and always say, if you believe a gossip, not even knowing the person being talked about, think about it . . . what does that say about you?

Paul

It was yesterday when we played in the yard. We played
hide and seek. You were the one that could never be found.
You were the one who played cards and could have always
won, yet now I know, you let me win too. I didn't earn it,
you just let me win. That was you, my brother, Paul.

Remember when you picked the mushrooms and
transplanted them, with hopes they would grow and
multiply. You were so hopeful they would, they didn't and
not until now, I wonder what that meant to you.
Under the lilacs I can see, I still can see you, planting those
mushrooms, so hoping they would grow. You just knew they
would, you told me so and with my childish wonder,
I wanted them to grow . . . I wanted them to grow,
if for no other reason, just because I believed in you.

I looked up to you, who you are, but I guess you didn't know
it then. We were never taught to show how we really feel.
Things of love were never spoken then. Things of love were
awkward weaknesses never spoken then. I knew, but didn't
say, you knew and did in your quiet, unspoken way.
You talked of stars and planets, rain and cars, you talked of
butterflies and birds, photos and telescopes . . . , you told me
some of your fears and many of your hopes. You were my
friend, in a world of solidarity. That was you, my friend,
my dear brother, Paul.

My admiration led me to your door of last days.
Your weakened body ashen and gray. I spoke to you of yesterday
and made you smile. Yesterday stood still, yet for just a
little while. All that was, did remain. We shared those
memories and it brought a smile, your smile made time
stand still, you remembered and your smile held yesterday
by memory's will.

It was yesterday when we played in the yard, we played
hide and seek. You were the one that never could be found . . .
today we look no more, today is the answer to yesterday's
unimagined destiny . . . , for now we know, you entered the
safety of heaven's gates and there you can be found,
peacefully resting in the love of our mother's arms . . .
where her children's waiting, eternal destiny is ever bound.

Paul . . . this writing is inspired by my brother, Paul, an extremely studious and intelligent individual. I looked up to Paul, as a child and admired him, as an adult. Paul was a very special part of my growing up years. He had an admirable quiet and gentle spirit. He was always planting something to make it re-produce something new or better and sometimes it did. Paul was several years older than me, so I tagged along behind him a lot. He never seemed to mind, actually he took his time to explain a lot of his interests to me and I loved it!! Paul loved art, so I learned to draw, he loved flowers and plants and to this day, I love gardening, he collected fine art and I too, collect paintings and limited addition prints. Paul's influences are a part of the molding of me.

Paul was a beautiful and unique person and will always have a special place in my heart and memories. Paul passed away with cancer. I will miss his vacant place in my life . . . until we meet again.

Alcoholism

Faded I, faded to a place I cannot stand. I reach for the false salvation of this need . . . , this untruth awaiting me . . . , awaiting to kill the pain of me, yet this need and pain it has given me to feed. This need . . . , 'tis waiting to swallow me, to swallow me . . . , 'tis waiting to swallow me . . . , will swallow me with the deadness of it's darkened will . . . , it's the deadness of it's darkened will, here to swallow me with pretences and promises to set me free, yet daily it swallows the me of me.

Daylight comes with promises made, promises of new day's light, new day's light so I can stand. I want to stand, oh, how I want to stand. I rise a weakened vessel with thoughts of hopelessness, yet promises wind through me still . . . , promises to conquer this forsaken will, this forsaken will, oh, I want to conquer this forsaken will.

I turn to greet my day, the sunlight blinding me . . . I pray no other will see, will see the hands that are a holdin' me, they are a holdin' me. Not one can understand, no, not one will see, not one will offer compassion's hope. Not one will look to me, look to the me of me with open heart, an open heart of compassion's stillness and care. No, they turn away, they turn away with whispers of doom, they say . . . , I should stay locked in a room. A shameful life is me, they say . . . , I want this monster that lives within, they say . . . , I purposely invite this darkness in, they say . . . , they whisper and say . . . , I control this darkened need, they whisper and say . . . , they say . . . , they say.

I pray for death's peacefulness, for the groaning of this lie is endlessly a beckoning me. Day and night I try my best, yet it hovers to smother the me of me. With every thought this need of darkness is endlessly, haunting me. It will not let me be, it owns the will of me. This darkened entity is smothering the soul of me, it shadows the soul of me.

The me of me cries out with silent screams of despair . . . , please don't turn your face from me, please see the me of me . . . , please see the me of me. I want to shine . . . , I can shine if I could free my will from this darkness imprisoning me. I want to be free from this darkness that is a holdin' me. Please, see the me of me. Look past the shadow that is engulfing me . . . , there is much beauty within . . . , that is truly me . . . , beauty is truly me.

Darkness comes and this bottle is a beckoning me. It's darkened, fermented waters reaching into the farthest depths of me, to steal the best of me . . . , to steal the light of me . . . , to keep me locked from the me of me. I want the me of me . . . , I want all to see, the me of me. I want the world to see . . . , God loves the me of me . . . , He loves the me of me . . . , He loves the me of me . . . and you equally.

Alcoholism . . . this writing was inspired by a friend that was an alcoholic. She was very well educated, she had earned many achievements during here life-time, yet she literally drank herself to death. She had the disease of alcoholism and it snuffed out her life. The inspiration to write this came from witnessing how people shunned this beautiful human being. I realize how difficult that it is to live with an alcoholic, yet I am talking about co-workers, friends and others in general. I saw laughter, because she stumbled to try to walk, I over-heard jokes of her drinking. She over-heard much of it and it hurt her deeply. I witnessed many kinds of cruelty towards this person and it cut right through my heart and it still brings a tear, as I write this. She was kind, caring, intelligent and a most giving person, yet many folks seem to ignore all of her beautiful qualities and only focused on her alcoholism . . . how sad is that? . . .

Angels Everywhere

Angels are ever there, to guide you through your day, and guard you in stillness of night. They speak with silent words, which slip into your thoughts. A moment of awareness you may not identify . . . it is your Angels and they are ever at your side.

God sent His loving messengers, assigned to you at birth. His Angels to protect and keep you all your days on earth. Angels everywhere, always showing that they care. You are not alone, for Angels work is never done. When you sense a warming presence 'tis your Angels· very near . . . a sudden thought of danger . . . 'tis Angel's silent speaking . . . a warning you will hear.

Look about . . . you will see Angels everywhere. A tiny little baby, with a face so sweet, the softness of a bunny or a hungry, homeless man with nothing to eat. A sudden act of kindness from a stranger's hand, at just a moment when you need one to understand. Angels have many faces to show you how they care . . . yes, they are ever near . . . , many times you have entertained Angels . . . , so unaware.

Angels Everywhere . . . life inspired this writing. I see so many people that are looked down on or scorned for this or that. I see homeless people or someone afflicted with a physical disability, as I am going from here to there in a busy day. I truly believe that some of these folks are Angels and we are unaware. I think that sometimes God places these Angels where they need to be to show us just how fortunate we are or to help us look out-side of ourselves with the need to somehow help those less fortunate. Some folks will pass by these unfortunate folks and scoff and judge, God sees this too. God may have placed these Angels in plain sight, with this effort to soften this audience's hearts. When I see one with less, if I cannot give to them, I pray for them and most times I do both. When something happens and we are rescued by a stranger's hand or kind words, no matter how minor the situation, just think, in all of these happenings, we may be in the presence of Angels, so unaware.

My Angels

I awaken from quietness of silent slumber, all things still, for morning is hidden by darkness' pause. My thoughts subdued by sleepiness, yet Angel's glow with lullabies, as pure, as mother's love.

Each day, as sun light calls, I relent to instinct's time, I awaken to a new day's promise, a new day to celebrate gifts and the Angels who come to stay, yes, Angels all about me be, Angels glowing with such loveliness and grace, sometimes . . . a loveliness and grace, I can only see.

Angels stand with welcome stance, ah beauty, so true and never vain. Angels I invite to my abode . . . Angels, at times, a special beauty . . . I can only know. Each time I try to choose, yet a new one pulls me near. Ah . . . I love this one best, yet this one I hold so dear.

I, but a mere, gentle one . . . , One who goes about my time with no complex cause. One who sees the beauty of Angels, each a lovely, visual fragrance . . . each, an answer to my heart's deepest call. A silent whisper that beckons with first glance . . . a vision of heaven's light, my Angels reach the tender part of me, as on my heart strings they play and dance. A dance to claim a place with me . . . a place with me to always be.

God sent His Angels to whisper a welcoming warmth, His silent whisper captures eternity's promises for me . . . my love for you will always be . . . my love for you will always be . . . by God's guiding grace and His Angel's love, this is now my heavenly destiny.

My Angels . . . this was inspired by a friend that collected Angel statues. This is a man that is athletic, couches basketball and works some with vintage cars. He shared with me that many of his male friends teased him about his fascination with Angels and his collection. I shared with him my thoughts of his love for Angels, which is . . . Angels are real and many are male figures. The love for God and His Kingdom has no gender favor and is a beautiful thing. We should all love everything about God's Kingdom and Angels are a huge part of God's Kingdom. I think that many people bow to the world's need to stereo type others. I am proud of this friend for not forfeiting his love of Angels, due to the narrow mindedness of others. I wrote this poem just for this friend and many of the thoughts in this poem came from his words, his heart, as to how he feels about his Angels.

This one is dedicated to you, Bob.

No Expiration

Today as I sit here looking at the reflection of me, it is aging I see, aging has come to stay, to stay . . . this is who I have come to be, this . . . now is forever me. Stillness, there is none, for time carries me closer to world visions of usefulness done. A time of slowing . . . a time of reflection, be it bitter or sweet, no matter, I have proudly earned a place in the world of the elderly . . . a place the world proclaims, as barely useful, as time honored and a journey now complete.

As I peer through these timeless eyes into a world of change, at times alien and foreign to the wonderment of me. A spark and need for growth is the light enticing this hungry wonderment embracing me . . . calling that need to grow and explore, a knowing that there is more . . . a yearning to search and stretch the alls of me. I want to stretch the alls of me. Curiosity captures attention's imaginations will . . . there is more I know I can be, this gifted desire to explore the alls God intended me to be.

God's gifts will forever be a part of me, forever be who I am supposed to be . . . who I am supposed to be . . . in my daydreams and reality I know I am not, yet all I am supposed to be. As long as there is breath in the belly of me, it is not finished. There is time to better the alls of me, the alls I am supposed to be, I still have work to complete, I want to complete what God has gifted me.

As I sit here and contemplate this history about me, the years of molding this person that you see, yes what you see is the working history of me. The toil, the triumphs, the tears and the cheers, the falling down and the crawl to stand again . . . the failures that brought devastation to the farthest depths of my soul, hopelessness feeding feelings that I can never win. Failures are illusions real, yet, failures can be lessons and the forerunner of each success, each tear a forerunner to my success. Failures are, but lessons meant to strengthen the endurances of me. My failures most time bowed to the successes I strive and earned to be me.

As I sit here with weakened eyes . . . ah, weakened by unforgiving and relentless time, I turn to look at my reflection and what do I see . . . an interesting one looking back at me. I look in the mirror and I do not see, I do not see an expiration date branded on the desire God gifted me, I do not see an expiration date, suggesting I cannot be more than what I see . . . God did not give an expiration date, so I will continue to be. He gave no limitations of expirations to dimly veil the forward growth of all those who are the realm of the precious elderly.

No Expiration . . . the inspiration for this writing comes from the way much of society seems to view the elderly or seniors, also the way many seniors view themselves. I believe that we are never too old for learning and pursuing new things, no matter one's advancing age. If anything, this may be all the more reason to seek out and pursue new goals and interests. The elderly have a lot to offer society. Society would be better if the wisdom of the elderly was taken more seriously. There is no better message of wisdom than a lesson that has been tried and trued. As long, as one has breath in the body and a sound mind, there is value in what that one can contribute; therefore there is no expiration date on learning and pursuing new goals.

What Death Means to Me

Death of the flesh is unavoidable for all. After birth it is the only certainty of our physical existence. Death of the flesh is not a selective process. No degree of intellect, wealth or a lifetime of goodness and greatness will afford us the privilege to be spared. It is the final destiny of all life.

I have pondered death a great deal. Death seems to have different meanings to different people. Many refuse to think on or discuss death due to fear. It is understandable and natural to fear the unknown. What I mean concerning the unknown is the actual process of death. I wonder, if one refuses to discuss death and/or ignore it, then will it not happen? I too, have some apprehension of that final act required of all living species, but I do not fear death. Am I prepared? I am sure that I will ask that of self until my moment arrives. I will spend my time diligently trying to be. I pray that my efforts will honor God.

I make all efforts to dwell on the positives of life. Why am I writing about a topic many consider morbid, unmentionable and negative? A topic many wish to avoid. I believe that death is a very important part of living. One should not waste one's efforts to mentally exclude it, yet one should plan for it along with all other increments of one's life. Embrace death with a job well done.

I believe in living and thinking on life with, as much zeal and realism, as I am mentally capable. Can one hide from or ignore the inevitable? Think on this . . . it is the answer . . . doesn't the wisest person look to all things with truth and plan accordingly? What hiding place is dark enough, far enough or timeless that renders an escape of our ultimate finality on earth? Have we not been taught since our beginning that life on earth, as we presently know it is temporary?

God gave us hope. He placed us here for a very special purpose . . . a purpose unknown to us. God's plan is for each of us to search and explore our gifts, to seek God's mysteries, for this is the key to understanding what life means. We are to seek to better mankind, be it micro or macro. God has linked all humanity together for the outcome of a common good. One may die not knowing all of one's gifts. One is not a failure, for one's journey may have been God's plan. On our journey to find our purpose, we travel many paths, change many lives and events along the way. Consider that God does not have one goal set for each of us, yet has given us many gifts to master and to share along this travel in time called life.

Many think of death, as the end. Death is the end of one journey, as if stepping from one plane to a higher, peaceful place of eternal beauty, a place of reward and rest, a place where tomorrow never comes for time is endless, a place where hope does not exist, for there are no needs. One should not fear death. One should cherish this life and prepare for a new and wonderful journey when this life is done.

What Death Means to Me . . . this writing was inspired by the fear that most people have of death. When I was very young, I too, feared death. I think it is the fear of the unknown that is associated with death that causes many folks to feel afraid. Death is just as sure, as our birth. After we are born, then death of the body is going to happen sooner or later. My thoughts are, why not be sure we are prepared for this event. I believe living a life for God and accepting His son, Jesus is that preparation. I personally do not believe in death. I do believe that the body will die, but the soul, which is who you really are, passes on. If one lives for God and accepts His son Jesus, then our soul will pass on to heaven. There is no fear in that. I feel a great and wonderful anticipation of my journey to my heavenly home. Yes, I have apprehension of the actual process of death of the body, yet when our souls leave this earth; it is a new and most beautiful beginning of perfection in all things. It is a natural emotion to grieve when a loved one passes on, yet if I know that person was a Godly person, this eases the pain of that loss. Death of the body is not the end; it is a new beginning for you, which is your soul . . .

The Many Faces of You

A face for this one, a face for that one, none the same, just the many faces of you. You are to that one this and to this one that, yet not the same to anyone, not to anyone . . . not even you . . . this . . . the many faces of you.

Trueness is eluding you unawares, for you are not true to anyone . . . not even true to you, no . . . you are not even true to you.

If you are this to that one and that to this one and none is truly you, then who are you . . . really, who are you? You are true to this one, yet not the same, as that one . . . are you really true . . . . are you true to them and you, when you show the many faces of you? When you agree with that one and this one does not agree with that one and you agree, then do you know who is really, truly you?

Which face is really you? You agree with all, although each disagrees, but differently with each one . . . , then which one is truly you? You agree to disagree with each one face to face, yet each one differently . . . this . . . the many faces of you . . . true to all, yet true to none . . . the many faces of you, the many faces of you are not even true to you . . . , for you live a life for only what surface shows . . . this . . . the many faces of you.

The Many Faces of You . . . this was inspired by people who are not true to themselves, so of course they are not going to be true to anyone. A person that is true to themselves takes a stand for something and stands by it, no matter the audience. It seems that some folks have no solidity in their core. They are this to that one and that to this one, yet never sure or strong to take a stand for anything right or meaningful, usually agreeing with all with-in listening distance. It is a kind of "go with the flow" to please the face that is looking back at them, even if it means hurting another. This is where the term wishy, washy comes from, I am sure. I think a lot of this comes from the need to win a popularity contest, which is usually fed my insecurities. Most of these folks are usually seeking approval from all and anyone . . . , which results in, "The Many Faces of You."

All relationships should own unselfish love, which is the only true, absolute love . . . this love will always be open to heart-felt forgiveness . . . this unselfish love, the only true, absolute love, will ever bring happiness and a peaceful wisdom to the heart that owns it.

All relationships should own unselfish love . . . this quotation was inspired by Cameron Speicher. Cameron is a very bright, intelligent and loving young man. Many of us do not think of younger people, as wise and compassionate, for many younger people do not learn these qualities until they are much older. Yet, Cameron has a genuine compassion for even those that have hurt him to his core . . . deeply to his core. I watched him forgive the nearly unforgivable, with a love that is usually only given from a more seasoned heart. I am so impressed with this beautiful young man, his kindness and gentleness surely touched by God's Angel's hands. No, he isn't perfect, there is no such temperament on this earth, yet this young man is blessed with a gift of wisdom only compassion has the power to give. His willingness to share and show this unselfish love, this only true, absolute love . . . inspires me with awe, as to who he is growing up to be.

All untruths will pass to the pits of darkened dust, yet all Truths will be known through the relentlessness of God's time . . .

Absolute Constant . . . Time

Is time the only absolute constant? It seems to me it is. We look through the veil of time and recall visions of our youth, as if it were yesterday. We turn around and our time has been spent. All things revolve and depend on time. Our world and the things in it have evolved with time, yet our conscious vision of life seems to be a step behind the constant movement of time.

It is wonderful to become independent . . . we use our time to earn and prepare for this freedom. Our lives are spent in deliberation of this use of time. The sweat and labor we give to time to become free of those timely demands . . . retirement is man's timely goal.

Time carries us on our journey, a journey that serenders with a finality to destiny's calling. This finality is summoned by the constant absolute of time. Time, a friend of our youth and too, a friend in our years of reaping. Some remembrances are with distant agony and some with a serene, melodic warmth, sustaining us on our journey's path . . . , helping us to choose, renew and grow with time's wisdom.

Yes, our vision of life is, but a step behind and when destiny calls the name of our loved one, then we look at time, the constant absolute, with bewildered reality. Where has time gone, how could this journey have traveled so fast nearly unnoticed 'till now? Time favors nothing, time favors no one, time never slows or stands still, time knows no demands of change, 'til destiny calls.

One can never escape the friendship of time and destiny's calling, for they walk hand in hand in our presence always. From our conception to our final destiny, time will always be our absolute constant. Time is God's gift to allow us all opportunities to be all He wants us to be . . . all we can be. Time offers a freedom to realize these gifts, to earn, to own one's space, to use and to spend it. Destiny is a goal . . . ; destiny is God's finality on earth. Time on this earth relents only to the bidding of God's plan, destiny's calling and the relenting of man's only absolute constant . . . time.

Circular Thinking

A wound to heal, an unjust act to define, this wound sure to steal my precious time. A wound an unruly heart did make, this wound I allow torment's web to contemplate. I give 'way my will to concentrate . . . I empower torment too . . . I search for this why in all I do, yet solutions only turn up unsolved again, my thoughts continue to circulate and all answers seem fleeting and hopelessly in vain.

Around and around my thoughts they go, my reasoning's illusiveness only echoes to answers of confusion's night-mare. My thoughts lost and laden with helplessness, lost in the poverty of logic's absence . . . trapped in circular thinking's prison of despair. Circular thinking is holding me there.

A new day awakens, as a new day will, this pain is with me still. I search to all questions answered and there . . . I again meet all answers with solutions still fleeting and seemingly unfair. No depth, no height, no wisdom to penetrate . . . no, not one thing to stop this circular motion inside my brain . . .

Ah, but 'tis I, that allows this endless siege, 'tis I, that holds onto the whys of this hurtful, tormenting need, 'tis I, who won't accept life's unjustness as it is, 'tis I, to give my will to the unanswerable questions of circular thinking . . . 'tis I . . . 'tis I, with God's loving wisdom, I realize the importance of me . . . 'tis I, empowered to stop this endless circular motion of thinking on the unanswerable why . . .

Circular Thinking... the inspiration for this writing came from knowing folks that seem to have a difficult time resolving hurtful events in their lives. Many times these individuals allow their thoughts to become consumed by all of the whys of the thing that hurt them. When this happens, it seems they allow the why of the event to go around and around in their thoughts, with no solid solution, which is circular thinking.

We all are a victim of another's cruelty from time to time, yet we can not allow these events to consume us. Expect that it will happen, then move on. If you are at fault, apologize and leave it there. Carrying hurt around with no resolution is a mental trap, which one can resist.

Take control of your thoughts, you own them.

I sometimes think that folks that are trapped by circular thinking, really think that they are the only person hurt by others. Not so, we all are hurt and sometimes with great cruelty, yet we cannot allow these events to consume us. This is what I am trying to say to those who find themselves continually re-hashing a hurtful incident. Unfortunately, unfairness and the resulting pain is a part of all of our lives... no one is an exception.

Consider What is . . .

Weigh what you have
with what you want
and what you will get
when you have acted
on what you want.

Consider what you have, be it good or a thought for better.
What is it that your heart desires that seems better than what is?
If you can change what is, then would you be better than what was?
It is a wise person, who considers what is and sees the good in it, if it is.
You, who will not see the good in what is, yet want more or better,
because you will not accept what is as the good that it is, yet will throw
what is away for the hope of what may be, yet what is may turn out to be
more than you thought it to be. What is may be best, consider all before
making what is what was, because of what you want.

Destiny's Light

I soar on to distant skies,
I make the stars a place to play.
I glide the moon beams, oh so bright,
never to know the end of day.

No longer will I look to skies,
with destinies of imagination's will.
No fears to stay my presence,
for time's essence
no longer holds my spirit still.

I laugh the laugh of freedom's heart,
I sing with choirs of Angels bright.
Oh joy; oh joy, my endless song,
for God's presence is destiny's light.

Doubt

The sun, "Oh, shine so bright, 'tis gladness a heart to bear."
"Oh, Spirit of me, a dancing go, a trouble I do not know."
The trees, the flowers, the sky above, no shadows lurching, so I can be.
I can be, all I have dreamed for me. A bird I see, oh, gliding so high,
I wonder, "can that bird see me, as it's gliding by?"

My tasks I do with assured strength, in confidence I do, no time to think.
I work so hard with heart of hope, oh, good my work, my heart does know.
My best I do, as I labor and toil, then suddenly a darkness come,
to steal away my grounded stance. 'tis enemy of goodness and calm,
'tis come to render my heart to spoil.

"Ah, I know thou, oh, too well, as you oft times come to dwell."
A silent thief, so quickly there, sure to render hopelessness
and turn a peaceful heart to much despair. "Oh, thief, oh, thief, to steal the best of me,
Oh, I will not loan the light of my destiny, for honor I have earned and I shall keep,
not to catch me, as asleep."

"Ah, I know too well, too well, my heart, my thoughts, you can not dwell."
I quickly turn away, thou unwelcome doom, I relent no place to stay. "Oh, doubt, oh,
doubt, your endless spoil, will melt away with time's cleansing thoughts."
A thought of truth, so I can be, a thought of truth to set me free.

The sun, "oh, sun, shine so bright, 'tis gladness a heart to bear."
"Oh, spirit of me, a dancing go, a trouble, I do not know."
"Oh, doubt, oh, doubt, I know so well, a place with me, you can not dwell."

Ecclesiastes 3: 1-8

To everything there is a season, and a time to every purpose under heaven:

2. A time to be born, and a time to die: a time to plant, and a time to pluck up that which has been planted.
3. A time to kill, and a time to heal; a time to break down and a time to build up;
4. A time to weep, and a time to laugh; a time to mourn, and a time to dance;
5. A time to cast away stones, and a time to gather stones together; a time to embrace and a time to refrain from embracing;
6. A time to get, and a time to lose; a time to keep and a time to cast away;
7. A time to rend, and a time to sew; a time to keep silence, and a time to speak;
8. A time to love, and a time to hate; a time of war, and a time of peace;

Eternity

Oh, body moan with wearing time,
thy youth to quickly to untwine.

No thing thy do, nor thing thy say,
thou lend my youth,
to elements of passing.
Thou deaf to plea,
demand my time to repay.

No sleep enough, nor fear enough,
nor wisdom great,
shall keep thou hunger at stay.

Thy every command, desire and toil,
not one of these make silent
thou erosive, endless spoil.

Oh, body so quickly pass away,
no bank will store, nor years to keep,
one breath, as passing day.

. . . yet thy soul . . . no age, nor elements,
nor thing, nor thought, nor height, nor depth
can diminish thy presence by death.

Oh, spirit, thy soul, with honor thou soar,
. . . ever on wings of eternal youth.

Expectations

What do I expect of you? Nothing more than I can be, for if I expect more of you than I can be, then what does that say about me?

Would it make a statement of my own insecurity? I think that it would speak that my heart feels less . . . to make you smaller, would I really feel blessed?

I have no expectations of thee . . . none that would feed an insecurity. I have no expectations of thee, for God loves us both equally.

I do have a wish for thee. I wish that you will always be better than me. I wish that all about you love will grow and peace of heart as only God can bestow.

If you fall by your own hand . . . I will not expect better of thee, yet I wish you to learn better than me. If you fall by your own hand, then reach up, for He will bring you up again. When I fall by my own hand . . . He reaches down to help me stand.

What do I expect of you? Nothing more than I can be. I have no expectations of thee, for God loves us both equally.

The most valuable quality of a life well lived, is a life lived by truth

Heaven's Race

I run, I run to His place of rest, a place I go when I've run my very best. I stretch forth my being to tempered ways. I test, I judge, I fight, I feel defeat, yet rise beyond the will of retreat. I go to paths where runners run, a body worn, yet spirit strong, ever to go on. My weakness brings me to my knees, yet I with stand the test of it, lifted with eternal strength. Wisdom bestows her gifts; therefore, I know my journey's land. I look beyond the darkened wall, no fear I feel, for light of faith leads me where runners run to keep me safe. The utterance within intercedes for me, an armor of light, the battle is fought before the path I see. I am not alone, this war within, the outward war I turn away, for I need not fight. I run to breaths of God. Oh, breaths of God, the shielding light.

I run with all, yet not all will a winner be. I run with all that is inside of me. I run with eyes affixed on Thee. I run with visions of His hope and strength for me. I run with all His gifts allow. I run to inner groaning's beckoning call. I run to earn a place at His feet, where rivers of life are crystal clear and those who sleep, I shall again meet.

I cross the line a tempered soul; I ran the race of mastery's goal. I cross the line of golden gates; I hear the cheers of welcome's song. I won, I won I shout out loud!! The music plays, as I stand in awe. The winner's crown placed upon my head, the book is opened and my name is read. A place to meet my destiny's will. 'tis I with tempered spirit a welcome plays. 'tis I who ran the race and captured the Master's prize. 'tis I who ran the race and won the grace of endurance's time. 'tis I who won a place at the Master's feet. 'tis I, 'tis I, I speak with no words. 'tis I, I joyfully proclaim as I humbly bow. 'tis I, 'tis I, oh, sweet Lord, 'tis I . . .

How High, Firefly

How high do fire flies fly,
I wonder, how high?

Oh, firefly, your light so bright,
penetrating darkness of heart and sky.

Fly so high, capturing the windows of me,
illuminating your course for all to see.

Oh, firefly, no beauty to compare,
You capture spellbound visions,
As you grace the night air.

Kiss the tree-tops where safety rescues you,
Sleep in restful stillness as morning softly,
sprinkles her dew.

Sleep in secret places 'til dusk's beckoning call,
Oh, dance firefly, soar and dip,
touching tree tops great and tall.

All wonderment exposed with sight of your light,
Oh, firefly, oh, firefly, luminous, awesomeness
of summer's night.

Oh, firefly, oh, firefly, how high do you fly.
I wonder, oh, firefly, how high do you fly?

How High Firefly... this poem was inspired one beautiful summer evening while sitting on my deck. I became fascinated by the fireflies and the fact that they fly so high. I had always assumed that fireflies fly near the ground. I lived in the woods and far away from city lights, therefore the fireflies light is all that I could see in the darkness. I was so spell-bound by the beauty of the fireflies, as I watched their magical flights. Watching them go far above the tree tops was amazing to learn and to watch. Some of the fire flies seem to fly so high, until I could see them no more. I was so caught up in the magic of watching the fire flies, I went inside to my keyboard and this poem came to be and it is exactly, as I felt at that very moment. To this day, it is one my favorite poems.

His Whisper

I, but a speck of life, I, a thought from Him,
I, a whisper He made, His whisper my life began.

He gazed to the stars; He placed them in my eyes,
He reached to the sun, then placed it in my smile.

He looked upon a daisy, He, then colored my hair,
He looked to the sunset, my cheeks, He placed it there.

He looked to His heavens, His wish a waiting there,
He smiled into my heart; He filled it with loving cares.

He looked all about me, the flowers He did make,
a lovely, blooming garden, just for happiness sakes.

He gave my heart His whisper, when I need Him close,
He speaks through the wind, He says, "I'm never alone."
I, but a speck of life, I, a thought from Him,
I, a whisper He made, His whisper my life began.

If We Would Change Our World

Everyone would love and respect old folks. They would not be lonely. Others would be interested in their stories of the past and appreciate the wisdom gained from years of living and learning. All their needs would be met. All children would have loving parents, regardless of their economic status. There would be no such thing as child abuse and/or neglect. Each child would have the nurturing that one needs to grow into a whole and loving adult. Each child would be blessed with at least one positive role model. Children would have all needs met. All divorced and unwed mothers would have the support system that is needed to feel confident to raise healthy children. Single parents would not feel alone and isolated. Single parents would have their basic needs met.

People would respect and appreciate animals as the living and loving creatures that they are. There would be no such things as animal neglect and/or cruelty. The feelings and needs of animals would be understood. Animals would be respected as a gift to man, not just a convenience for man.

For those who say there is no God, because they cannot see, feel or hear Him . . . they would wake up their senses and realize God is all earth's seen and unseen, felt and not felt, heard and silent beauty. To look into the face of a new born baby is to look into the face of God. He is in the loving smile that is meant just for you. God's signature is the colors of all things He has created. He is in the sounds of rain, waterfalls, His whisper is the wind. He can be heard with the sounds of all of the animals, the peaceful sounds of a happy baby. He is the smell of clean air after it rains, the smell of newly cut grass, flowers and good food. God can be felt when the warm sun touches one's face on a cold day, the cool breeze on a hot day, the summer rain on ones skin, the softness of an animal and the hug from one that loves us.

People would have caring and respect for others. No one's value would be judged or measured by physical appearance, economic status or mental abilities. There would be no gossip, lies abuse and/or neglect. All races would blend in harmony. People would like who they are and in turn have a free heart to like others. People would pray for others instead of being critical. The collective human goal would be to cause no harm for another, but have real compassion and always willing to help.

If we would change our world . . . it would not be a perfect place, for troubles can build strength. The things that we would change are attainable, yet many times people will not open the windows of their hearts to see, therefore the changes we will make in our world will have to come from within you and me.

Each of us, as humans with common interests and pursuits of happiness, must accept the responsibilities of friendships with all considerations and not falter.

Lost

Bewildered by the world I see, a world of unwelcome to the spirit of me.
I turn to walk away, yet footsteps of darkness follows, to smother my day.
My days once full of sun, are of darkness each and every one.
I ask you Lord, "deliver me from these hands that are holding me."
My strengths have weakened and forsaken my peaceful will.
No rest for me, for I walk this valley of darkness still.
"What is the answer, Lord, what am I to do?" "I seek all answers from you."
Another day of unrest, another day I have tried, yet failed my test.
Another day to wonder in confusion's land, another day I seek your hand.
As I sit here a bewildered soul, I seek your light to restore my eternal glow.
Restore the glow of my tired heart, restore me Lord, I'm unsure where to start.
Bewildered by the world I see, a world of unwelcome to the spirit of me.
Oh, spirit of me grieve not, for I will make a stand, He will make me whole again.
I search for the good of me, no rest 'til I reach my tranquil destiny.
"So, Lord, take me by my hand, give me strength this day to stand."
I wait on all promises made; I wait and will not falter with Faith.
Faith, oh Faith, I look to thee, for I know your spirit is carrying me.

Love

Be a friend to all. Be not a judge. With open love and caring, we are to love others. The greatest achievement of all is to spend one's energy mastering the gift of love. It is a test of one's wisdom and strength, yet with work and time one can achieve the reward and peace of it. Is it possible to love all others? Probably not. What then? Turn away without thoughts of bitterness, give this to God. We can only understand in part the mysteries of God, therefore those things we cannot master, give to Him, walk away and do not look back. The love I speak of is the love of our neighbor. Who is our neighbor? All those who cross our path in life, all those we know about, all those we hear about, all those of our world. Can one really love most all others? Think on this . . . one can either love or hate. One will be what one allows to grow in one's heart. Negative judgments are from hate. A place of strife and pain, a place of strife and pain for self and/or others. This is not of God. Love for all is God's master plan. God has bestowed to us many degrees of loving. Some we will love less, some more, yet we can love. The ability to love others is a gift. A gift to others and you. We can walk the straight paths of God with first steps of love.

God made each of us with His absolute love. Each of us are different with His understanding. Judging another is to say to God . . . His timing is wrong or He is wrong and knows not what to do. To judge another in anything is to appoint oneself in God's place. Judging others is to judge God. I am not speaking of God's elect, the elders of the church. I am speaking as a neighbor, your neighbor.

Do I love all others? No, but I earnestly try. A seasoned person of God will strive to master the gifts of love for others, which allows a greater understanding, patience, compassion for self and others with rewards of peace. At one time I owned the heart of a fool, with thoughts to condemn, words without forgiveness a bitter heart. There was a time I cherished myself righteous, empty heart. I suffered much turmoil and pain. With God's patience, work and time, I learned the peacefulness of a loving heart. I daily work to perfect it. My energies are given and tested for what is good. Love is the greatest gift from God. God expects nothing of you, but love. If one loves, then most all in one's life will fall into place, as God intends. If I know anything . . . I know this . . . I can love. I cannot love all the same, yet I can love.

My thoughts on Our Differences

I could talk about individualism. Webster defines this as, a belief in the primary importance of the individual and the virtues of self reliance and personal independence. I will talk about individualism, yet in terms of our differences. Think on this, they are actually the same. The world focuses on the differences of others and how we seem to compare ourselves to others to justify who we are or a possible need for change. This can be good, yet many times this is done with absolute negativity. Negative comparisons is what I am speaking of.

God created all things to blend into a balance of perfection. Our differences is a recipe designed to blend together to form this harmonious balance. If one will think on this, then one will understand this truth. God loves us all equally and gave each of us a special uniqueness to prove this is so. He gave us special gifts all our own to master and to share. God's wonderful gifts for each of us was never meant to be a tool used to compare our special uniqueness to or against another. We compare ourselves to others, with the result of self or another at the negative end of this conclusion. This seems to be the norm for us.

Consider that each of us is a piece of a puzzle and it takes the pieces of others and their differences to make the puzzle complete. Some pieces are of different color, shape, size, yet is one piece more important than the other? No. With out each piece in its exact place the puzzle would be incomplete.

God created each of us different; therefore we compliment each other in the workings of life. None is lesser or greater, because one is different. A blend of our differences results in a single equality. Individualism is God's plan when employed, as He intended it. Take our gifts of differences and help those who lack one's own qualities, in turn that one can reciprocate their gifts to form a complimentary union.

The relationships of our world could build and become stronger, if we could accept each one's own special qualities. Each could know a peace and contentment within, with the realization that it is good and natural to be different. There would be less expectations and more acceptance of self and others.

God made the puzzle of us with an art of perfection. Each piece linked together, as it is intended will bring a balance to one's life, to one's world.

Never Alone

When we are in pain we all feel alone. Whatever the cause, to whatever degree the pain, we all feel a solitary existence. When we face that place of despair, we can be in a crowded room, alone, or in the presence of just one other, yet feel that no one is really listening, understands or cares.

Many believe that God is closer to those who have many blessings of richness from this world, a fulfilled life, good health, yet this is not so. God is closer to those with nothing than to all those who have much or all. There seems to be a great misunderstanding, especially to those who have so little. We live in a materialistic world, a society which measures a person's worth by the value of one's outward possessions. In turn many seem to believe that only those with the abundance of the world's goods, good health and joy are heard by God . . . the only ones worthy of blessings. Be it a rich one with much or a beggar with nothing, God loves all equally.

We are never alone, for God is ever with us. In a time when we dwell in a place with feelings of isolation, He is holding us and His love is stronger still. With my search of His truths, I have learned that His love is strongest for those of low degree, for at that time we need Him more. He knows every tear. He is our Creator; therefore we are connected to Him in all things great and small. He sees all things, He knows all things and His love is always there.

Pain can be an emotion of isolation. Pain disconnects one from the awareness of the loving intent of others and God. Pain can take us to a place of darkness, although the sun is warm and bright, a place of sadness, a place void of happiness and sounds of joy are only a reminder of ones loss.

No matter how low, how lost, how empty, how much despair, God is there. Just that thought is to hold His hand . . . hang onto that thought until He helps you stand. In one's darkest hour, He is always there without invitation. Be it one of the world's wealth or a poor one in any degree, God is closest to all who go to the lowly place of pain. Pain is but a season, a temporary place, a place where you are never alone, for God is there ever holding you.

One Breath Away

Fear not the end for me, cry not tears of vacancy's agony.
Stand not and seek my echoes in the stillness of familiararity,
For I went to distant spaces of Truth's promised finality.

I did all I knew to do, while on my journey's earthly path.
I fought the fight of life, in all I won, for wisdom gifted me,
For my triumphs and trials great, never to be undone.

Dry your tears for me . . . I had been patiently waiting this promised destiny. I worked and diligently prayed, awaiting my turn to see the Angels welcoming brigade.

Someday you will join me in God's Holy land, Someday you will know and understand, I am here waiting to once again hold your hand. One breath ends earth's temporal course, this . . . His plan, shares not earthly remorse.

Cry not tears of anguish and sadness forlorn, for this was my destiny, given with first breath, the moment I was born.

My first breath opened earth's time, spent doors. My last breath beckoned awaiting Angel's absolute love, cradling my spirit, now I am complete, as new, as the awaiting white dove.

Cry not for me, for I am now watching over you. One day time will relent to your earthly destiny . . . with one last breath, Heaven's gates will open wide . . . and there . . . awaiting you . . . I will be.

Personal Evolution

I think of time in terms of evolution. Our own personal evolution. Time is an increment ever in motion, a forward motion with or without us. Our personal time is meant for growth, hopefully, to work towards growth of positive goals, revelations and outcomes . . . yet that is up to you. You decide how to use your time . . . in the long run you will live out the results of your decisions, which is your personal evolution of time.

You are the author of your goals and achievements. There will be many paths you have set, but at times must change course when least expected . . . a time of uncertainty and confusion, yet time even in these darkest valleys is good, if one will look for the lessons of it and apply these to one's life for strength and wisdom . . . this bringing an evolution of more strength and wisdom.

Time does not slow or wait due to your likes, dislikes, needs met or unmet, traumas or joys, as you work through this life. Events of yesterday cannot be erased, yet time allows a new day of changing you and events passed. Your script can be re-written, for time allows this with it's forward motion. One cannot erase what was, but one can re-do what was to a renewed place in time.

Time . . . our space, our invisible space of mapping our journey good or bad. Time is macro and micro, it can be used for your personal likes and dislikes, which decides how you use this wonderful giving, forgiving and ever moving forward motion of your space . . . your personal evolution

Our bodies and souls are an hour glass. One's body will diminish, yet hopefully, one's soul will grow. How we daily map our personal evolution determines the quantity and quality of our destiny. Not all have the privilege of choice in things of the physical world, yet we all have the freedom of choice, as to what we allow to grow with-in us at some level.

What do I think of time? Most times we don't consider what it really is. It is a gift to us for our own personal evolution. I come to realize that time is ever moving forward and we are physically regressing, as it moves. As time moves forward our bodies and all physical things of this world declines and wastes away. Spiritually, joyfully and physically we move in opposite directions, therefore I work to make the very best of every moment while I have breath with-in me. I am not suggesting any of us to be obsessive concerning the fleeting of time, yet a wise person considers how this gift is used for the best outcome of self and the good of those around us . . . , which is our personal evolution. Think on this . . . all will diminish and grow towards something with the fleetingness of time.

Sometimes

Sometimes, I see the sun so bright,
but sometimes I don't.

Sometimes, I do a good deed,
yet sometimes I won't.

Sometimes, I have the patience of Job,
then sometimes, without thought, I say, "no."

Sometimes, my light shines ever bright,
but sometimes, I don't let it show.

Sometimes, I see other's needs,
sometimes, I just let them be.

I am so glad that sometimes,
God is not like me.

Sometimes, is not the way of God,
for He is always the same.

He doesn't love me just sometimes,
He loves me simply always.

Tears

A tear . . . a crystal clear fluid of the heart,
By God's command, caught by Angel's hands.
A tear . . . a treasure earned with each new drop,
Each tear forever sealed in God's book of gifts
To ever bestow.
A tear . . . a confession of the heart,
Not one unnoticed or lost, for in memory's
Book, each one counted and sealed,
Proclaiming God's own presence,
As each tear by Angel's hands is gently saved,
For this . . . God's loving remembrance of you.

Time

Time, oh time, where did you come from
Where will you go? I follow you each morning,
Into weariness of night.
Oh, time bid me each days
Newness of light.

Oh, time can you show me your face
Or make visits to my dreams,
Oh, time are you my protector
Or are you my enemy unseen?

Time, I am here waiting for you,
To show me what's next in place,
Ah, but it's you, it's you time, for
You even own this moment's grace.

Ah, but I turn and see, it is me, time,
It is me. You are a gift God
freely gave to me., a gift of Thee to me.

Tomorrow

One never knows what lies in the morrow. The gift of today is your eternity on earth, for tomorrow is, but an increment of time hoped for . . . it is not a promise. Our time here is, but an unspoken, borrowed gift. Each moment of today is an awesome gift allowing us a time to pause, to ponder, to search accomplishments and needs . . . an ability to mend, to change, to grow in the empowering, newness of now. God allows us only now and the awareness of this. This, in itself is a gift to encourage us to stretch to be all we can be today. Imagine . . . if we used every moment for the good of self and others . . . how much could we be . . . think on this. Should tomorrow come, then yesterday's accomplishments will be the richness stored in one's heart . . . the knowledge that we can reach a little higher and continually be more.

What does tomorrow mean to me? I, as most of us do, many times take it for granted that I have tomorrow. Lately, I have been giving this a great deal of thought. What if I gave each moment, each circumstance, each event of today, within my ability, to be what God wants me to be, for I only have now to achieve what is intended for this moment.

Tomorrow may not come or in the morrow a change may be . . . rendering me unable to be what I am today, therefore I have learned to inhale the beauty of my moment's gifts, my free will, my awareness and understanding of today.

I wish to give; I wish to console, I wish all good deeds from me. I wish to hold a candle bright to light the path for thee. If I do all things good and hold a candle to light the path for thee, God will instill a peaceful heart and a showering of blessings to me from He and thee.

Treasures of the Heart . . .

One can have anything in one's heart, but how does it get there? Everything that one thinks and speaks, which manifests one's behaviors is stored in one's heart and grows. Each one decides what stays to grow. What one speaks is from the treasures of the heart. If one speaks with love and kindness, then love and kindness will be stored in one's heart for recall. Each word or act of love will continue to multiply. As is with the darkness of bitterness and strife. If one is full of bitterness and strife, then one's thoughts, words and behaviors most times will be with a temperament of bitterness and strife. You are what you allow in. What you allow in will multiply. What already is will multiply. What new thing one allows will add to what is.

Think on this . . . for this is truth. God gave us the gift of free will. We are free to choose what we allow in our hearts. If one thinks and sees the world with a heart of bitterness, discontent and hate, then that will be the treasures of one's heart and will be what one thinks, speaks and is. If one chooses to filter out the negative thoughts and retain what is beautiful and good, then one will think, speak and be that which is beautiful and good, with a loving radiance, which is the light of God.

The heart that holds bitterness and strife is a heart of darkness. That one most times will see their world through darkened windows first, for that is the treasure of this one's heart. There is no light there, for God is not there. For those who will not allow darkness to stay, then that one will beam with the radiance of God's light. Think on this . . . can one be what is not in one's heart? No, one will only be what is the fruits of one's own heart. If one is discontented with what is in one's life, then look to the treasures of the heart, for what is there may be the reason for one's unhappiness. Most times it is. Most times those who allow darkness to dwell and grow in one's heart do not like themselves. How can anyone like the emptiness of a darkened heart? One's self image comes from the inside out. We are to love ourselves, yet love will not stay in a heart of darkness.

Do I have darkness in my heart? At times we all do, yet what we allow to stay and grow will determine who we are. Sometimes it can be a battle to push out or let go of negative thoughts or events. One must let go to keep the glow of light in one's heart. Some days it seems impossible to filter out the hurtfulness of this world, yet it is possible with time. Yes, sometimes it can be a struggle or a fight, yet with awesome rewards of peacefulness. The more one brings love in the heart to grow, the more one sees their world as a place of light, a place of peacefulness, a place of joy and all of these with the ever-growing warmth of God's light in one's heart.

True Friendship

When life has tested you beyond your strength . . . your knees bend with heaviness of sorrow and weight of tears . . . your friend is there holding out a hand, so wanting to help you to regain yourself again.

A true friend's love is a rare treasure for sure . . . . a treasure sure to continually endure. Life can bring an unexpected storm, a turbulence to take us off our peaceful course. A true friend knows this and offers a selfless understanding for a love, a friend who's hope and heart has been tossed and torn . . . a soul bewildered, broken and forlorn.

Friendship is one of the truest loves. True love knows not it's self . . . only the need of a friend. Friends will always give treasures of a loving friend's heart. Patiently waiting in the silence of time, waiting to share the pain . . . with an endurance rendering a love so kind.

When life is a test beyond all strength . . . a true friend is there to hold your hand . . . to help you regain yourself again.

What is Forgiveness to Me . . .

To forgive is to release one's self from bondage. Be it verbal, physical, intentional or unintentional, all have been a victim of another's cruelty. One does not need to remain a victim, forever in the grips of pain and anger with an everlasting, unsatisfied need for justification that magnifies and multiplies with time. This need can erode away the gentleness and peace in one's heart, the stillness of contentment in one's thoughts, the softness of a loving expression on one's face, the freedom to grow beyond this pain and the strength and wisdom one earns with this growth. With each thought of the painful deed, hurt and anger will grow, keeping one bound to this person and pain. Forgiveness disconnects one's bond with this agony. There are those who will question the truths of what I say here. That is good. For if one questions, then one is not closed off to the possibility that there may be freedom in forgiveness. If one is absolute in thinking this is not worthy of one's efforts, then one is not ready or does not wish to be free of the corrosive bonds of hate.

When I think of forgiveness, I think of Romans 13:17 and 13:21: Recompense to no man evil for evil and be not overcome of evil, but overcome evil with good. I believe God is saying in verse 17, "do not return evilness for evilness received." Second God is telling us, "do not allow the evilness of another overcome you, yet reciprocate that deed with a deed of goodness, such as prayerful forgiveness for an act of unkindness. Only good will reap good. Bitterness is a form of hate in any degree. How can good for self come from the act of hate? Think on this. It is the answer. For harboring hurt, anger and any form of resentment and bitterness is to harbor hate. There is no freedom in hate. One will free oneself by refusing to reward the unkind act with wasted time and energy dwelling on all of the never to be answered questions. The why of any unkindness can be a trap that takes us on a trip of endless disappointment and possibly self persecution and blame. An unforgiving heart is locked in time. One will not grow beyond the unkind act 'til one forgives.

God has a plan, a safe route for all things in one's life. God's plan is for us to maintain a balance in all things. Forgiveness will remove torment and bring a peaceful calm. Forgiveness restores a balance between good and evil. One may never forget another's cruelty or unkindness, yet one can forgive. The reward for a forgiving heart is the freedom to learn and grow beyond one's pain.

When one removes the negative energy from oneself, a more positive you can flourish. Forgiveness is a healer. One has the power to mend one's own heart through the act of forgiveness.

Patience

Patience is a tool, a timeless calculation with a determined will for the best outcome. Patience is a disciplined love, desire and self-obedience for what one believes to be right. It is a gift from God that can be difficult to manifest when needed. Patience is a Godly love that is learned, then given by one so disciplined.

Patience is a test of self, a test of selflessness. One can turn one's back on anything, yet those who are patient will endure with a timeless calm, earning strength and peace by working and achieving the final goal. Patience is a silent, solitary endurance with time. The prize . . . more strength, patience and love.

Patience can be given with silence, words of encouragement, an absence, a constant presence, yet always with some degree of love. Patience and love are as one. I ask you, can one be patient with no degree of love? It is all in God's plan, one only has patience when there is love . . . another way for God to give balance to life.

Our greatest example of patience is God. God is love. With His love He teaches us an endurance, which brings calm, structure and peace to ones soul. With that love He offers us a timeless calculation with a determined will for the best outcome . . . for oneself . . . for all humanity.

What is Peacefulness . . .

Peacefulness is a reward, a gift from God for following the straight path. One can only know peacefulness by living a life of truth. Peacefulness is a nourishing calm, a freedom, a strength, a place of contentment, a place where an awesome love grows and the ever-abounding need to give love away. The gift of peace is a promise God keeps when one gives one's best efforts to practice His righteous ways. Peacefulness is an inner strength, a freedom to walk the path of life with no fear of the unknown, an assurance that all is or will be well in the worst of times, the ability to know unimaginable joy in the best of times. One who practices God's love and disciplines will earn a strength and calm, which will appear to others, as a glowing warmth of welcome, an inviting spirit of genuine friendliness, magnetically drawing others near. One who has earned this state of peacefulness will display a loveliness, a gentleness, a true and earnest will to give. This willingness captures even the hardest hearts, although it may be but a moment in time. Think on this. Are not the most impressive persons, those who are a loving rock in the midst and in spite of all the world's calamity?

Peacefulness is the most sought after state of well-being. The world offers many activities and products designed to bring one peace, yet at best one will only gain a shallow, temporary state of artificial peacefulness. The reward of true peace only comes from God. This peacefulness must be earned with work, then rewards of wisdom bringing the fruits of peacefulness. It is available to all. It is free. It is a promise from God, therefore with efforts and time peacefulness will be.

What is peacefulness to me? To be at peace removes obstacles, allowing an awakening of freedom, granting an awareness of love all around me that only God can bestow. His peace allows me freedom from the world's ugliness, a shield to walk my path in life, victorious over the pain of this world, be it spontaneous or with time. A place of freedom allowing patience and understanding of my weaknesses and an inner calm of disciplined strengths. God's peacefulness opens one's heart to self-love. With love of self, there flows a need to keep that which is good, rid self of that which may cause one to stumble and the wisdom to know the difference. Peacefulness is, as an open window to self and the ability to see one's own soul without obstacles, therefore the freedom to feed my being with this nurturing of love, strength and wisdom which guides me to a place where peacefulness will grow, in turn a need to share this place with others in need of peacefulness.

The peace that I speak of is a reward, a gift from God for following the straight path of truth. Our life is, but a vapor in time, so quickly passing its course. One can live our given moments from God in a state of true peace, if one will.

What Life Means to Me

Life is a gift given to me by God. There are those who would argue that knowledge, yet I will not debate this inner wisdom. This is my reality, which the Highest Entity of the most powerful, absolute love has embedded in my being. I do not question the origin of this gift.

The gift of life is to be cherished, yet many days I fail to acknowledge the preciousness of my own heart that beats within me. I take it all for granted.
Most times I look around me and it is then I see, hear and know that there is so much power in what life really means . . . it's value is only measured when it's purpose is given away.

Many things of life will be a mystery for a season . . . a question. Life is a quest to find the answers to my reason . . . the reason I was created by One so perfect. I am in awe at times when I consider that I was chosen to have life and to dwell here for God's purpose and time. I am in awe at times when I gaze at my own reflection and pondered His love so pure when He created me. My quest is to seek and fulfill His hopes for me. He created each of us with this same special love. With absolute adoration and love He gave each of us life.

What does life mean to me . . . today as I sit here, I can't answer this question with a poetic voice of wisdom, because my life has many meanings to me. I can say this . . . "it is an energy to be shared for the good of those around me." My life is a gift to be given away to others as I journey through my space, trying to perfect me with the Father's guidance. Hopefully, I will have fulfilled some of His purpose for creating me. I will spend my time earnestly trying to be a reflection of His ensample . . . the pureness of His gift of instinct to love I can only imagine, yet I so want to be at least a part of it.

What does my life mean to me . . . that will only be answered when God ends my time here. Only then can it be known, for the value of my life will be measured by the reflection of my peaceful heart . . . due to the fruits of what it meant to others . . . and to my loving, creator, God.

Where God is

I try to picture where God is concerning all of one's mental states. We, who know Him, know His presence in times of joy, yet what then in times of trouble? I believe God only dwells in positive places. By that I do not mean only one's mental state of happiness, joy or even our place of peace, for one can be at a lowest level, a place where one's soul feels anguish, closed off, yet the Spirit of God is closer than all other times. One may be in a place of anguish, yet God is there and always in the light. I know these truths, for He is the same always. One's spirit will lift up to seek open places of light and joy during one's darkest hour . . . more than any other time . . . , for this is where God is.

I have given this a great deal of thought. When one has the spirit of God dwelling within, it is only natural to seek where God is. One's spirit will seek Him more so in one's darkest hour. One's soul may be with great anguish and feelings of absolute despair. One may emotionally flat-line, contained in a vault of anguish, yet the spirit of light will seek to nourish one's soul. It is seeking deliverance to where God is. One's soul will cry out to be in God's light . . . one's spirit will answer.

I try to focus on the positives of all life. As I have said before, I know our world is troubled, yet I seek the positives in all life, for that is where God is. There are many others who have chosen to focus on the comparisons of rights and wrongs and all unmet resolutions of this world. This is good, for we need to find a resolve for our troubles. I believe the answer is to seek where God is. This is where the positives in all life dwell, be it the wind or materials understood or to be understood . . . it is the energy of light, the light energy within all who know Him.

Have I experienced pain and despair? Yes, as we all have. Has my soul felt alone? I think so, yet my spirit, the awesome spirit of all things positive and possible fed my mental state with a flicker of light to show me where God is. The light in me will be there when nothing else remains, when at a place where one's soul is at a lowest level of existence. It is then one's spirit will take one on the upward, wide open place of light . . . to where God is.

Who Took the Yellow from Me?

Who took the yellow from me? The yellow is the light of me. The light of me to light my path, so I can be . . . that was the yellow in me. I look at dawn to find the yellow in me, I look 'til dusk only to know it is still gone and I cannot be . . . with no yellow in me.

I search my world to find what took the yellow from me. I turn to him or her; did they take the yellow from me? Was it this or that or an unfortunate circumstance that took the yellow from me? I search to fault, to question all things validity.

I, once so full of light. I, so joyful and full of life. I had the yellow in me. I was all I could be, 'cause I had the yellow in me. What a wonderful way to be, full of yellow that was me. I had the yellow in me. All things good was all I could see, 'cause I had the yellow in me.

Now darkness has in-camped my heart with window shades of gloom. Where is the yellow in me? Who took the happiness of me, which was the yellow in me. I turn to all I know. With dismay I wonder, "how can this be?" "I have no yellow in me." In all this despair, a darkened path is all I see.

Finally, I look to Thee, "where is the yellow in me?" I reach up to take His hand; He helps me so I can stand. He opens the eyes of me. He shows me all I need to see. It was not he or she or unfortunate circumstance that took the yellow from me. Blindly, I would not see, it was me!! It was me that took the yellow from me. I took the yellow from me, 'cause I did not trust in Thee. Oh, Faith, it was I who turned away from Thee. I took the yellow from me.

Again, as new, as mornings first light, filled with Truth's promises, I see, now I see what took the yellow from me. It was me, for the light of He is the yellow in me. It was me who did not look to Thee, so I could keep the yellow in me. He is the yellow in me. Finally, He and me, we restored the yellow in me.

Yesterday was as if yesterday. Ah, where did our time go? You were the one, so quiet, so bright. The one to earn merits of intellect. You the studious one. All I know is what I know. What I know of you is, one so intense with all life's questions of why. A searching of nature's secrets. Secrets not to be hidden from your curiosity. A curiosity of searching, which has brought you to this destiny. I wonder . . . , did your wondering intensity, understand this destiny?

It was yesterday we played hid and seek in the darkness f our country home. You were so good at finding us. You knew where shadows guard. Shadows guard a child's hiding place.

A Collector be

I travel my journey of life with eyes to see, ears to hear, my sense of touch and smelling the fragrances of living all around me. With all of these my spirit collects essences and I grow, yes I grow with daily searching to walk my path . . . my journey of time.

I sort out the things of least desire, I ponder things great to be, then collect all I need to be me. I see the beauty in every simple thing God gave . . . I relish in it. I collect it. I store it for now and/ or later, I store it as a part of me, it becomes me, the me you see.

Ah, I want to be what I want to be, so I collect what I want me to be. The things that make my spirit grieve, these things I don't want to be me, so I shut them away once I learned what I need to see . . . away from me, so they cannot become a part me. These undesirable things . . . I cannot allow to be me, so I put them away . . . forever out side of me. I work to keep undesirables out side of me.

I love the sunshine of my soul . . . I search all to bring light to me, I collect things and people to give, restore and maintain the light in me. This is who I work to be . . . a collector of the lighted things. The Godly lighted things.

Darkness comes as darkness will in people, places and all. I have much to collect from this dark valley still, for lessons to be learned in this sluggish valley of time. Things to collect in this sluggish valley of time. I learn to soar as I grow to the light . . . I collect the wisdom of it. I collect the wisdom of it, as I soar to God's ever beckoning light.

I, a collector of all God's simple things, for complexities are not of He. Complexities He allows . . . allows us to see, so we can choose. I am a collector of what I want to be, the things I want to be me. The good of all I collect and keep . . . these become a part of me, they become who I work to be . . . this is what God has said to me . . . I can be whatever I want to be, a collector with my soul open to what I should collect for me. This is the balance God has given me.

I collect the things that form a happy me, so you can collect my essence bright . . . therefore you too, a collector be. I emit my collected light . . . it is me . . . this is me, I wish to share the collection of me . . . I wish to share the light of me, the best of my collection I wish to share with thee . . . , for this radiance, I understand . . . we are all a collector be.

Angel's Songs

May the light in me shine for the light in you,
For the light in me is Angel's songs in all I do.
May I reflect the pureness of truth, so you can see, Angel's light in me,
then your light shall grow brighter with this essence of peace.

May you hear the whispers of Angel's hearts, understanding your journey's song,
Angel's sonnets of love, with visioned silence, a seeking whisper all day long.
May the road before you be blessed with an assurance of your Angels and mine,
For 'tis this, a road well traveled, with the eternal hope of heaven's endless time.

May grace be in abundance when your head will not rise and your back is weak,
May you hear Angels softly calling you, as they cradle you in your sleep.
May you rise above all challenges great, Angels ever holding you from the
darkness of defeat.

May the light in me shine for the light in you,
For the light in me is Angel's songs in all I do . . .
all I do is Angel's songs, I wish to share with you.

Corinthians 13: 1-13

Though I speak with tongues of men and Angels, and have not charity, I am become as sounding brass, or a tinkling cymbal.

2. And though I have the gift of prophecy, and understand all mysteries, and all knowledge; and though I have all faith, so that I could remove mountains, and have not charity, I am nothing.
3. And though I bestow all my goods to feed the poor, and though I give my body to be burned, and have not charity, it profiteth me nothing.
4. Charity suffereth long, and is kind; charity envieth not, charity vaunteth not itself, is not puffed up.
5. Doth not behave itself unseemly, seeketh not her own, is not easily provoked, thinketh no evil;
6. Rejoiceth not in iniquity, but rejoiceth in the truth;
7. Beareth all things, believeth all things, hopeth all things, endureth all things.
8. Charity never faileth: but whether there be prophecies, they shall fail; whether there be tongues they shall cease; whether there be knowledge it shall vanish away.
9. For we know in part and we prophesy in part.
10. But that which is perfect is come, then that which is in part shall be done away.
11. When I was a child, I spake as a child, I understood as a child, I thought as a child: but when I became a man, I put away childish things.
12. For now we see through a glass, but then face to face: now I know in part; but then shall I know as I am known.
13. And now abideth faith, hope and charity, these three; but the greatest of these is charity.

Psalm 116: 1-10

I love the Lord, because He hath heard my voice and my supplications.

2. Because He has inclined His ear unto me, therefore will I call upon Him, as long as I live.
3. The sorrows of death compassed me, and the pains of hell gat hold upon me: I found trouble and sorrow.
4. Then called I upon the name of the Lord; O Lord, I beseech thee, deliver my soul.
5. Gracious is the Lord, and righteous; yes, our God is merciful.
6. The Lord preserveth the simple: I was brought low and He helped me.
7. Return unto thy rest, O my soul; for the Lord hath delt bountifully with thee.
8. For thou hast delivered my soul from death, mine eyes from tears and my feet from falling.
9. I will walk before the Lord in the land of the living.
10. I believed, therefore have I spoken: I was greatly afflicted:

Romans 15: 1-5

We then that are strong ought to bear the infirmities of the weak, and not to please ourselves.

2. Let everyone of us please his neighbor for his good to edification.
3. For even Christ pleased not himself; but as it is written, The reproaches of them that reproached fell on me.
4. For whatsoever things were written aforetime were written for our learning, that we through patience and comfort of the scriptures might have hope.
5. Now the God of patience and consolation grant you to be likeminded one toward another according to Jesus Christ.

Kindness speaks volumes to another's grief.

What is Hope . . .

Hope is something hoped for, yet not seen. Hope is an imagined destiny, an object or place desired in one's heart and mind. Hope is a need for one's imagined destiny to become a reality. Hope can carry one on a journey of success or defeat. The hope that I will speak of is one of a positive desire.

Hope is a mental state of promise. A state of joyful anticipation for things to come. A hopeful heart is patient. A heart that knows no limits in time. A hopeful heart will bear all elements of time to gain strength, as each moment passes. True hope never dies. When all the world answers in defeat, true hope withstands all doubt.

God's hope is first thoughts of faith . . . something hoped for, yet not seen. Faith is the steadfast knowledge that what is hoped for will, with no elements of doubt come to be. God gives us a gift of hope and faith to allow us the joy of tomorrow's promises.

One who carries hope in one's heart will bear all things. When the world has taken one's last inspiration, hope will manifest and help one to rise again. The knowledge of hope in all things is an armor of continuing life. Hope maintains a balance between positive direction and loss. Hope gives positive direction. Without hope one would be lost.

What is hope to me? Lately, I ponder the meaning of hope a great deal. I, as most all others hope for many things in life without thought of this act of hope and what it really is. I know that positive hope is God. Hope is a gift of love from God. Hope is a flicker of light given to light our destiny. When I try to understand hope, I do it best when I try to imagine my life, all life without the spirit of hope. Life would be meaningless. Life would have no reason or direction. Without hope there would be no motive or mental vision to grasp allowing the need and ability to move forward in time. Hope is a guide, a spirit of truth and promise to carry one to a better place. A guide to where God is. For God is the light of hope in all things good.

What is the Light . . .

Many ask, "what is the light?" I am sure that the light has different meanings to different people. Is one right as to what it is and another wrong? No. We are all unique and not one of us will perceive any one thing the exact same as another, yet the light is the same in all things. Each of us is created to be different, therefore rendering a compliment and/or an extension to another's understanding, yet there is, but one light source and that will never change.

I can say without doubt that the light in all of us is of God. I will not debate this. God is the light and there is, but one God. This is a simple truth. Those who wish to debate this do not know Him; therefore how can one debate a thing that one has no knowledge of? The light is the Spirit of God living within us.

The love and compassion that one feels and expresses, is manifested by the light that lives within us. The light in you will hear another's joy or pain, as the rest of the world sleeps unaware. The light in you will reach out to assist in times of troubles or rejoice with another in times of joy. The light gives the gift of insight, awareness, a sharing; therefore the light in you will feel whatever is for another. One of the light will shine with love and compassion for all, as one standing on a hill top, for all to know and see, yet many without understanding.

What is the light to me? It is the love of God.

Seeds of life

Oh, seeds, did fall upon the ground, did tumble, a rugged path
the mindful wind did make.
A nook to rest, the earth to take.

Oh, seed, oh, seed, the sun, the rain, the soil to penetrate.
New life to bear, an hungered, a better one for mother's sake.

A sprout to grow and flourish still, to reach for skies at daylight's will.
Oh reach so high and stretch so tall, your beauty's birth at sun lights call.

Oh, flower, a flower take thy glorious stand. Kissed by sun and moon and rain,
to shine a miraculous life all new and grand.

But a moment blessed,
oh, time, a stealing element. Oh, time, oh, time,
'tis hidden blessings you have sent.

All dried and changed,
yet new again, to pick, to keep.
Ah beauty . . . never vain,
a gift of time quietly unique. You cruelly steal away,
. . . some will whine and weep.

Oh, flower, yet a first thought, a soft and lovely whisper
of One who made you known.
A seed of life, to flourish, to grow,
a blossoming fragrance all your own.

Oh, flower, oh, seed of life . . .
but a vapor granted, so like the seed,
a thoughtful, lovely whisper manifesting life a new,
so like the life of seeds and flowers, so like the life of me and you.

Ecclesiastes 5: 18-20

18. Behold that which I have seen: it is good and comely for one to eat and drink, and to enjoy the good of all his lobour that he taketh under the sun all the days of his life, which God giveth him: for it is his portion.
19. Every man also to whom God has given riches and wealth, and given him power to eat there of, and to take his portion, and to rejoice in his labour; for this is the gift of God.
20. For he shall not much remember the days of his life; because God answer him in the joy of his heart.

What does today mean to me . . .

Today is a celebration of life a new. Today is a gift of time that God has allowed. An opportunity to renew, replenish or to seal one's own heart or that of another. A time to reflect on yesterday, a time of hope for tomorrow, a time to live today with a new celebration of life for the prize that it is.

Today is an offering of love from God to right the wrongs of yesterday, to rejoice in all things good. The opportunities to mend, rebuild or do away with that which has hindered good. Most times we take today and its renewed promises for granted, not considering the given empowerment for the betterment of all things.

Think on this . . . for all those who are lost, it is a new day of hope. For those who are hurting, a new day to mend. For those who have nothing, a new day earn, gain and achieve a dream. For those who have much, a new day to give. The day of birth is a day of rejoicing a new life. The day of death, is a day to celebrate rebirth. What more can God bestow to us than the promise of today?

I ask you, what hope is there in yesterday? Yesterday is spent, and never again will be. What hope is there in tomorrow? Tomorrow is not a promise, but a wish, a hopeful desire. Today is a true gift from God. His promise of our only hope and potential to give or to take of yesterday and tomorrow is in today.

What does today mean to me? As I sit here, I think on this moment and fully realize it is my only promise of time. I ponder my use of today and the realization that there is no promise for tomorrow, therefore I know I must value this gift of time and make all efforts to make all things new. Today is a gift that God allows. A promise to celebrate life, today's life for the gift that it is.

Freedom's Will

Glide the heavens far, go with freedom's will,
capture me in awe, with your beauty's light.
My Love, of solitary uniqueness,
this place in my heart will never be stilled.

A whispering of wind, soft like flickering candle light,
a solitary thought, manifested by your presence.
My Love, bid me more than moment's grace,
the sights, the sounds of your eternal magnificence.

I turn to reach, to touch, your beauty to ever keep, yet,
but a vapor lent, you are God's perfect plan. My Love,
resting ever in my heart,
soar in heaven's light, going before to ever be.

Glide the heavens far, go with freedom's will,
capture me in awe, with your beauty's light.
My Love, of solitary uniqueness,
this place in my heart will never be stilled.

Let loving words of wisdom sting the
staleness of another's heart.

Timeless Butterfly

Oh, butterfly of solitary elegance, a
warming grace all your own.
Glide into the windows of the heart,
speaking to the spirit as you dance.

Butterfly of awesome, illumines array,
a colorful fragrance magnifies your presence.
A camouflage of safety, as only God can give,
kiss the wind as it carries you on your way.

Oh, butterfly, too short the time you spent,
oh, glide the blossoms, the grass, the heart of me.
I reach, not wanting to let your beauty go,
yet with understanding life's journey . . . you lent.

No thing, no sound, no sight, no knowledge great,
will fill the heart with your timeless space.
Oh, butterfly of solitary elegance,
a warming grace all your own.
Glide into the windows of the heart,
speaking to the spirit as you dance.

Oh, dance, to memory's moments of light, Oh,
butterfly too short the time you spent, I reach,
not wanting to let your beauty go, Oh,
butterfly of solitary elegance.

Proverbs 15: 13-23

13. A merry heart maketh a cheerful countenance: but by sorrow of the heart the spirit is broken.
14. The heart of him that hath understanding seeketh knowledge: but the mouth of fools feedeth on foolishness.
15. All the days of the afflicted are evil: but he that is of a merry heart has a continual feast.
16. Better is a little with the fear of the Lord than great treasures of trouble therewith.
17. Better is a dinner of herbs where love is, than a stalled ox and hatred therewith.
18. A wrathful man stirreth up strife: but he that is slow to anger appeaseth strife.
19. The way of the slothful man is as an hedge of thorns: but the way of the righteous is made plain.
21. Folly is joy to him that is destitute of wisdom: but a man of understanding walketh uprightly.
23. A man hath joy by the answer of his mouth: and a word spoken in due season, how good is it!

Treasures of the Heart . . .

One can have anything in one's heart, but how does it get there? Everything that one thinks and speaks, which manifests one's behaviors is stored in one's heart and grows. Each one decides what stays to grow. What one speaks is from the treasures of the heart. If one speaks with love and kindness, then love and kindness will be stored in one's heart for recall. Each word or act of love will continue to multiply. As is with the darkness of bitterness and strife. If one is full of bitterness and strife, then one's thoughts, words and behaviors most times will be with a temperament of bitterness and strife. You are what you allow in. What you allow in will multiply. What already is will multiply. What new thing one allows will add to what is.

Think on this . . . for this is truth. God gave us the gift of free will. We are free to choose what we allow in our hearts. If one thinks and sees the world with a heart of bitterness, discontent and hate, then that will be the treasures of one's heart and will be what one thinks, speaks and is. If one chooses to filter out the negative thoughts and retain what is beautiful and good, then one will think, speak and be that which is beautiful and good, with a loving radiance, which is the light of God.

The heart that holds bitterness and strife is a heart of darkness. That one most times will see their world through darkened windows first, for that is the treasure of this one's heart. There is no light there, for God is not there. For those who will not allow darkness to stay, then that one will beam with the radiance of God's light. Think on this . . . can one be what is not in one's heart? No, one will only be what is the fruits of one's own heart. If one is discontented with what is in one's life, then look to the treasures of the heart, for what is there may be the reason for one's unhappiness. Most times it is. Most times those who allow darkness to dwell and grow in one's heart do not like themselves. How can anyone like the emptiness of a darkened heart? One's self image comes from the inside out. We are to love ourselves, yet love will not stay in a heart of darkness.

Do I have darkness in my heart? At times we all do, yet what we allow to stay and grow will determine who we are. Sometimes it can be a battle to push out or let go of negative thoughts or events. One must let go to keep the glow of light in one's heart. Some days it seems impossible to filter out the hurtfulness of this world, yet it is possible with time. Yes, sometimes it can be a struggle or a fight, yet with awesome rewards of peacefulness. The more one brings love in the heart to grow, the more one sees their world as a place of light, a place of peacefulness, a place of joy and all of these with the ever-growing warmth of God's light in one's heart.

Romans 12: 9-18

9. Let love be without dissimulation. Abhor that which is evil; cleave to that which is good.
10. Be kindly affectioned one to another with brotherly love; in honour preferring one another;
11. Be not slothful in business; fervent in spirit; serving the Lord.
12. Rejoicing in hope; patient in tribulation; continuing instant in prayer;
13. Distributing to the necessity of saints; given to hospitality.
14. Bless them that persecute you: bless and curse not.
15. Rejoice with them that do rejoice, and weep with them that weep.
16. Be of the same mind one toward another. Mind not high things, but condescend to men of low estate. Be wise in your conceits.
17. Recompense to no man evil for evil. Provide things honest in the sight of all men.
18. If it be possible, as much as it lieth in you, live peaceably with all men.

Psalm 51

Have mercy upon me, O God, according to thy lovingkindness: according unto the multitude of thy tender mercies, blot out thy transgressions.

2. Wash me thoroughly from mine iniquity, and cleanse me from my sin.
3. For, I acknowledge my transgressions: and my sin is ever before me.
4. Against thee, thee only, have I sinned, and done this evil in thy sight: that thou mightest be justified when thou speakest, and be clear when thou judgest.
5. Behold, I was shapen in iniquity; and in sin did my mother conceive me.
6. Behold, thou desirest truths in the inward parts: and in the hidden part thou shalt make me to know wisdom.
7. Purge me with hyssop, and I shall be clean: wash me and I shall be whiter than snow.
8. Make me to hear joy and gladness; that the bones which thou has broken may rejoice.
9. Hide thy face from my sins and hide all my iniquities.
10. Create in me a clean heart; O God, and renew a right spirit within me.
11. Cast me not away from thy presence; and take not thy Holy Spirit from me.
12. Restore unto me the joy of thy salvation; and uphold me with thy free spirit.

Corinthians 2: 7-16

7. But we speak the wisdom of God in a mystery, even the hidden wisdom, Which God ordained before the world unto glory:

8. Which none of the princes of this world knew: for had they known it, they would not have crucified the Lord of glory.

9. But as it is written, Eye hath not seen, nor ear heard, neither entered into the heart of man, the things that God hath prepared for them who love him.

10. But God hath revealed them to us by His spirit, for the spirit searcheth all things, yea the deep things of God.

11. For what man know the things of man, save the spirit of man which is in him? even so the things of God knoweth no man, but the spirit of God.

12. Now we have received not the spirit of the world, but the spirit which is of God; that we might know the things that are freely given to us by God.

13. Which things also we speak, not in the words in which man's words teacheth, but which the Holy Ghost teacheth; comparing spiritual things with spiritual.

14. But the natural man recieveth not the things of the spirit of God: for they are foolishness to him: neither can he know them, because they are spiritually discerned.

15. But he that is spiritual judges all things, yet he himself is judged by no man.

16. For who hath known the mind of the Lord, that he may instruct him? But we have the mind of Christ.

Aging

Does the spirit age in comparison to one's body? I have pondered this and my conclusion is no. One's spirit does not age as we understand the aging process. There are things that will remain a mystery in our appointed time here, yet God gives us this simple understanding. I believe that one's Spirit matures, be it positive or negative, this is determined by one's gift of freedom to choose one's own path in life.

One's body is a fragile vessel, which requires utmost care. In this piece I am not speaking of those who went on before the aging process due to any cause, yet an early passing is, but a reminder of one's unknown hour and the need for daily preparation. Only God knows the mystery of that limit.

As one ages, one becomes more aware of one's own physical changes, either believing or without thought that the Spirit is maturing, yet is ageless. One's body will age until death, yet the Spirit is timeless. Does that mean that we never really grow old? Yes, I believe it does. We are timeless, for we are not the body, but the Spirit. Just as one builds a new house to dwell within . . . it will need repairs as time evolves, then eventually erode to destruction, some structures sooner than others, yet all will have an end. Our bodies too know an end, yet our Spirit will endure forever. This is one of God's simplest truths.

When many think of death they think in terms of finality. The body is gone, therefore all is gone. This is not so. Death of the body is not a finality, yet a new beginning. This body is not me, for I dwell within this body. When one looks at another, one is not looking at who one really is, but a vehicle, a tool enabling humanity to continue on. One's body is a gift from God, yet it is not one's true identity. Only a world without Truth's understanding moves on unaware of one's own identity.

What do I think of my aging process? I think it is a part of the natural human psyche to wish to stay physically youthful. In this respect, I am no different than many others. Do I want to dwell on this earth as we know it in a youthful state? Of course, yet this is not God's plan. One's body is God's hour glass. One can determine one's nearness to completion in this world by this time machine. As I age, I look upon the world differently, yet the same as in my youth. Differently, because my Spirit has matured. I understand my body's eye is but a looking glass for me, my Spirit. I watch the body change and grow with limitations, which bring natural apprehensions, yet I see the world with a matured youthfulness. Do I fear aging? No, for I understand it.

Balance

A balance in one's life is a gift from God. It is a peaceful place of reward for striving to do what is right. God gave us a free will to choose how we will live our lives; therefore our choices will either bring a balance or an imbalance.

God made all things to work within perfect balance, when done as He intended. To achieve and maintain balance we must follow the straight path. God's truth is the straight path. When one integrates His truths in all aspects of one's life, the results will be a peaceful balance, which also reflects onto those around us.

God is love. With God in one's heart, one will express love in most all ways one thinks, speaks and responds to the world around us. The spirit that dwells within us will manifest and produce our outward person. We are the treasures of our hearts.

Can there be a balance with out love and truth in one's life? Hate is a destroyer of love and truth. Will negativity, if allowed to seed and grow, manifest a balance in one's life? Negativity is, as being on a teeter-totter alone, there is no balance, because it is not of God.

God is absolute love and truth. Absolute love and truth is absolute balance in all things. We with all of our weaknesses cannot know and express absolutes, yet when we learn to apply God's love and truths, we can know a peaceful balance within.

In my life, what is balance to me? Oft times is seems elusive, a continual struggle, yet that struggle allows me the privileged continuance to walk the straight path of love and truth. God's balance is a place of freedom. The freedom to realize with wisdom, God's gifts and the freedom to use those gifts to stretch and grow, to learn to be most all that He intended for me.

Change

Change brings new dreams, pursuits of untouched promises: treasures of the heart only imaginations knew. Change is offerings: offerings of possibilities true.

Change . . . be it a wish, a challenge, an unexpected turn, an unsettling force, a pause in time, a change of course: seemingly a thief that interrupted you.

Change . . . oft a stranger disrupting tranquil slumber: awakening one from silent stills: a quiet wedge of walls, which threatens a solid will.

Whatever is or brings about: if hope or enemy unannounced: change serves truths with elements of time. Change brings time's wisdom and blessings to thine.

Change brings new dreams and pursuits of untouched promises: treasures of the heart only imaginations knew. Change is offerings: offerings of possibilities . . . possibilities just for me and you.

We all must make our own place on this earth, for we are our own vessel, guided by the hand that we reach out to, as the spirit we have chosen, we follow . . .

Defined by Jesus

Don't define yourself by the mistakes you have made. Many times folks walk life's journey carrying the burden of past mistakes on their backs. They can't seem to do enough, say enough, love enough, live enough to make up for the wrongs of yesterday. This burdensome guilt shrinks the true value of who they really are.

Every one alive is guilty before God. We have all sinned against God. According to God, "no one sin is any greater than another," yet we brand this deed or that deed more wrong than the other. We brand others and our selves more wrong, depending on the sin. Think on this . . . who are we to disagree with God?

Guilt is the burden that we carry or place on another. God uses guilt as a messenger to alarm us that we need to talk with Him and change something. God never wants the burden of guilt to stay. Guilt can be a friend if we allow it to help rid ourselves of sin, yet an enemy when we won't let go. We are never to place the burden of guilt on any other.

Jesus died for our sins. Every time we pray and ask our Heavenly Father to forgive us, the Angels in heaven rejoice, because we are all new again. We are clean, as if our sinful deed never happened. The problem . . . we won't forgive our selves. It is a sin to carry the burden of guilt, because it is a lack of faith in God's promise. Think deeply on the reason Jesus died on the cross. Stop . . . think on this.

As the song says . . . "while He was on the cross, I was on His mind. He looked a head in time and He knew me. Ponder this . . . He looked ahead in time and He knew me. What greater love is this? He died knowing my mistakes before I was ever born. Who am I to doubt Him by defining myself through my past mistakes. Who am I or you to define any one by their past mistakes. Jesus died so we can be free and renew ourselves through Him. Define yourself by Him, through Him, because of Him. Try to imagine . . . on the cross He knew me . . . He looked a head in time and with our heart felt plea . . . He defined you and me.

Experiencing

We have knowledge and understanding of a subject, yet we don't have the emotional experiencing to make the subject real to us. It is, as if having a blue print for a house, we can see and understand where everything goes and that it is a house, yet until we are living in the house and we emotionally experience living in the house, then it is just a drawing of a house.

This same theory is true with people, their understanding and growth. We can be taught anything, yet it is a subject of knowledge only, unless the emotional part of us is added to that knowledge. Once the emotional part of that knowledge is added, which is experiencing, then the subject is real, heartfelt and is a personal learning experience.

What I love is, once we have experienced something and made it real to us, then we can continue to experience and whatever is can grow, as long as we feed it with each new experience. Each experience of anything will help us to gain knowledge and grow. This is a cycle. It is God's plan for our leaning process.

This cycle can be painful or joyful. Both with the result of leaning deeply. Experiencing anything is our guide and treasures in life. Negative or painful experiences are lessons. We have knowledge of painful events, yet unless we experience them, they are things we here about or know about, yet until we experience them, they have little meaning, for the subject is not a personal reality. Painful experiencing can bring much needed knowledge and strength if applied to our life for the good. Joyful experiencing, such as falling in love, the love of a new baby, puppy or whatever it is that makes you have a joyful heart, can grow by allowing your emotional self to be open and giving. In turn knowledge will grow as well.

Experiencing anything helps us to know the reality of that subject. Our intellect and emotions work together in a cycle of experiencing to allow our knowledge to grow and become our reality. We all have a free will, therefore it is our personal choice as to what we will accept, experience, learn and grow to be our reality.

What does this mean to me? I have pretty much always had the knowledge of this theory, yet it was not a subject that I pondered, until I had an experience with a friend that turned the light on for me, so to speak. I was trying to explain something to this person and she just didn't understand. I found myself getting very impatient, then it was like a light coming on, I understood why she couldn't understand. She had never experienced what I was speaking of.

Flowers

Flowers dance to breeze's will, dance to God's breaths of harmony.
Dance to radiance's glow, dance to Angel's hands a helping grow.

Hands a tending with gentlest love, hands surely guided from above.
Hands sow and plant, hands with earnest care, emit a silent essence of life's
new hope, with time . . . , awaiting each newborn awe to bare.

With help from sunlight, and moon, with help from whispers of God's
own breath, the call of sunlight and caressing dew. With help from a
garden Angel . . . , bound to manifest, she tends to God's flowering earth.
She tirelessly nurtures each one 'til a flowering birth . . . , a flower
reaching to the light of sky. She spends her time working with hands of
love, for she understands . . . , God's gifts of flowers are sent with love.

She goes to the garden while dew is sleeping still, 'tis sleeping with drops, as tears, fall
silently with no command or will. She joyfully tends to God's mystery . . . , a mystery
just for the delightful awe of you, me and she.

Each flower a gift. A magical, mystical life uniquely designed all new. A gift touched
by God's own breath and Angel's hands. A glimpse of heaven's radiance . . . , a
message sent on Angel's wings, a radiant language of heaven's colors and fragrance.
Heaven's secrets . . . , through flowers . . . , delivered by the loving care of Spring time
Angels, He has sent.

Flutter by Butterfly

Good morning, pretty butterfly,
I'm watching you as you flutter by . . . ,
As you flutter by, I'm watching you,
Pretty butterfly.

Hello, little butterfly, so tiny,
So small, doing what butterflies do,
As you flutter by. So much power . . .
the essence of you, holding this
Spell bound audience of one,
as you flutter by, little butterfly.

Hey, busy butterfly, can you see me too,
as you flutter by, busy butterfly.
Dancing in the windows of me,
to my heart strings harmony,
Oh, busy butterfly, flutter by.

Good afternoon, graceful butterfly,
the sun and you are one,
ah, so radiant, sweet butterfly,
So unaware of beauty's sake,
so unaware of vanities fair,
As you flutter by, graceful butterfly.

Good night weary butterfly.
Flutter by to hide in slumber,
As hypnotic dusk captures you,
In darkness you will not flutter by.
Sleep now, oh, weary butterfly.

When daylight peeks at you,
dawn calls, 'tis time to taste the dew.
Ah, grand appearance you make,
As you flutter by, sweet butterfly.

Oh, flutter by, sweet butterfly.
One more day is spent
And a new one to begin,
As you flutter by, sweet butterfly.

Grieving

Each tear is answering to the desperation of my soul. Imperfections, you may have had many, yet not, for our love was a blanket, a gift of blindness, which stayed us through the years to beyond heavens gate. Heavens gate opened for you too soon.

Each sound, each scent, each moment allowed me, is but one more breath closer to where you are. My love . . . each breath bidding me to stay, yet is spent in the silence of was . . . therefore relenting my time.

Your presence echoing near, yet as invisible as Angel's whispers. I search for you in all our familiar places, but only grasp your essence in my soul . . . my singular existence engulfed in the sweet memories of you . . . drowning in your absence.

Time made it's beckoning call . . . you answered and are gone. I walk this journey of life, which was two . . . how quickly spent the time you lent . . . how quickly spent . . . this time you were lent.

Have You Ever

. . . seen a Hummingbird as it is sitting still?
Have you ever heard the owls,
As they call out under the full moon?

Have you ever listened to the rain,
As each drop freely falls on the roof?

Have you ever watched a baby at play,
And realize that place of peace?

Have you ever held a friend,
And shared their pain or joy.

Have you ever watched the lightening,
And wondered what it really is?

Have you ever looked to the sky,
Hoping to see God?

Have you ever stopped to listen,
And hear His voice so clear?

Have you ever looked around you,
With peaceful understanding . . . He is there?

Have you ever stopped to realize,
God speaks through all these things?

Have you ever seen a Hummingbird,
As it is sitting still?

Heaven

I dreamed of heaven far away,
Beyond the whitest clouds and the bluest skies.

I dreamed of gates all gold and shining,
Of Angel's wings effortlessly flying.

I walked along the paths of green,
So rich with color, like I have never seen!

No sky above, so ground below,
So clear and bright, all seems to glow.

How I got here, this is so . . .
Just a blink, oh now I know.

I used to ponder how it would feel,
To leave my home of earth's great toil and zeal.

Now, as I glide along these awesome shores,
I seek no more at "ole doubts" door.

I **Did Not** See

I passed right by, I did not see,
I did not look at thee, so I did not see.
I hurried by in blindness, of all, but me,
I could not see, I was so full of me.
I hurried by and did not see.

I hurried by, oh, a late me, no time to see,
As I hurry on . . . , time is fleeting me.
You standing there, I did not care,
No time to care,
I did not see you standing there.

Years of haste, no time to waste,
I never had no time to waste.
Ah, a day did come, I looked to see,
I turn to see, through tears I see . . .
You no longer wait for me.

I passed right by, I did not see,
I did not look at thee,
No, I blindly did not see.
I turn to see, through my tears,
All those years you waited for me.

I passed right by, I did not see,
I did not care, I did not see.
Through all those years, I did not see.

Now, I see, I finally see, I have time to see,
for you no longer wait for me, now I see . . .
Through all those years you needed me.

A Little Butterfly

Hello, Little butterfly, I am watching you as you swirl on by.
Do you know I am watching you with an amusing delight.
I wonder, little butterfly, do you watch me too, as I'm watching you?
Are you watching me, little butterfly with a spellbound curiosity.

I am curious, little butterfly, where do you go when it rains?
Do you hide in secret butterfly places where butterflies go?
When the rain drops come down do they find you there
Or do you hide with butterfly cover, resting without a care.

I wonder little butterfly friend, is there a flower you like best
Or do you taste them all teasing, tickling each flower, as you feast.
Pretty butterfly how do you know, which flower is meant just for you?
Is it in the color, the fragrance or maybe it is the morning dew.
Does the morning dew call to you, as it glistens in the morning sun?
Showing you each flower, as you taste each one by one.

One more day is done, say good night little butterfly to the sleepy sun.
When shadows come and daylight dims to darkness everywhere
Where do you sleep, as the world rests all the while of you unaware.

Do moon beams reach down and cradle you in each ray of light,
cradle you in butterfly secret places all through the night? I wonder little butterfly,
will you return again or will I see another butterfly friend.
Good night little butterfly, for I am going to sleep, as I too relent to darkness' call.
Sweet butterfly, you capture my thoughts and now my dreams.

When daylight peaks through darkness and we say hello to the morning sun,
will you answer the call of the morning dew, as it glows with invitations
and promises of a grand new day that is meant just for you.
You will see me watching you as you dip and sour entertaining this audience of one.

Love is . . .

Love knows not it's self, for it is continually seeking another's needs.
Love is never blind, it is the guiding light through all darkness.
Love is never vain, for it knows only the inner beauty of another.
Love is always first, it does not wait until all else has failed.
Love never slumbers, it is there ever waiting to give.
Love is a guide, to lead to a place of peace.
Love is constant, for it knows no pause.
Love is wise, for it knows all truths.
Love has no limitations, for it knows not time, distance or space.
Love knows not it's self, for it is continually seeking another's needs.
Love is God . . . that yearning in our hearts, to show the world who He is.

Messages Without Words

When I look around me what do I see . . . unspoken messages capturing me. The flowers, the trees, the sky . . . messages without words, at times no sound, messages of Truth abound. I search the colors and He is there, I feel the breeze 'tis a whisper, an unspoken message of His grace . . . no words, yet I am aware. "Sunlight, oh sunlight, do guide me, 'tis messages so bright, no words need be, for His warmth is the surrendering of me." A heart need no voice to hear, to know, to feel, to see, for all around are unspoken messages . . . His loving presence knows all needs. His lovely whispers are all things good . . . for all around I can see, His messages without words ever speaking to the spirit me.

More Than We Can Be

God made us to be more than we can be. He gave each of us our gifts to pursue and master, yet at the mastery level, we are not yet all we can be.

When I think on this, I realize that each of us can spend a life time reaching to achieve our interests and talents, yet if we live a full life expectancy, we will not be all we can be. If our physical bodies did not fade, we could continue on learning and growing towards the gifts that God gave us, yet would we ever reach the maturity of His gifts? I don't think we ever would. I think He gave us the ability to master one gift, then pursue another time and time again.

There are those who do not search their gifts, yet that doesn't mean that God did not bless them with gifts. He did. He gave everyone a free will to pursue, search and stretch to accomplish what He laid before them. If a person will not try to discover themselves and their own uniqueness, which is their free will, this is a refusal to grasp the gifts awaiting them. Sometimes I think that this is a form of a self made prison. God's gifts of interests is the life inside of you, which reaches out to most things around you. Something draws you to certain things, with thoughts, such as, "I like this or that or I would like to do this or that." That is the gifts of God. If you don't use them, then you may wither and die an unhappy, empty shell.

Each of us, no matter our intellectual level, all have gifts. If we are at the lowest level of mental capabilities, there is something we contribute, possibly involuntarily. Every person has a soul and an ability to enrich the workings of life for self and/ or others.

We are given the gift of life. With the gift of life, God gave us many talents, abilities and desires to search and achieve, yet if we continue to pursue all things of our interests, which is our gifts, we will not achieve all the gifts God gave us. He gave us a natural curiosity enabling us to find who we are and what makes us happy. His love for us has no limitations. Our bodies will pass away, yet the true capacity of His gifts will ever be unspent. Our talents, desires and abilities are endless. We will always be . . . more than we can be.

Open thy heart, open thy mind, consider the unspoken thoughts before the deliverance, for your audience may bear a wounded soul.

My Heart Called to You Today

My heart called to you today, and there, I found you in the treasures of my memories. I saw your smiling face, looking back at me. I listened to the laughter we once shared and dwelled in it.

My heart called to you today, and there, we talked of life and endless promises lent by yesterday's seal of time. I called to you today and your answers flooded me through memories of yours and mine.

My heart reached for you today and you touched me. As we walked the lane, the daisies nodded as if in remembrance too. Vacancy's will, cannot stay the presence of you.

My heart called to you today, and there, I reached out to you . . . , with open arms of love's awareness. I sensed your warming presence . . . , for we shall forever behold the nurturing, quietness of devotion's answers . . . , silently speaking through our heart's endless memories . . . , my heart called to you today.

My True Love

Finally, I know a love with no limitations. One who gives all I ask with a timing for the good of me. He is there with just one thought . . . I need not pause. Heart aches have been many, yet this time I know my heart so true. This love is meant to be . . . to be strong through eternity.

Some say, "I am foolish, just believing in fairy tales of yesteryear." Some say, "my heart is radically misplaced." Some say, "this too will someday fade." They say, "my love is, but a passing phase, only good when I am in need and never a certainty." Some say," I am wasting a good heart on the hopelessness of imaginary dreams."

My love is so misunderstood by many, scoffed and scorned. "He is a wondering dreamer, never a house to call his home, no address, never in just one place," they have pointed out to me. "He, a great philosopher, a spiritualist, one of great intellect, yet no proof of all written and said". "His charismatic smile and promises of a love so true, none of this is meant for you," they say, they say. "He is but an intelligent dreamer," they say, they say.

They do not know you as I, for if they did, they would love you too. They would see the wondrous happiness in my heart, then know all you say and do is true. I wish they could see and know you as I, a love so strong and great, for me you were willing to die . . . for the love of all lost in unworthiness . . . unworthiness of others and I . . . Jesus, my true love, for me and you . . . , allowed himself to die.

Our Motives

One's motives is an increment of one's deepest self. Our motives are our self revelation. A motive begins with a thought, then the reasoning of that thought, while searching the best beneficial outcome. One's reasons for the expected outcome is one's motives.

With time, one's motives can rarely be hidden. With time our motives reveal who we are. One's motives are a window to one's heart. We should ponder our motives in all things. Our motives can be used, as a tool to guide us on a positive course in life. If one's motives are for the good of self and others, then one will gain a self-fulfillment and an endless peace in one's life. With an awareness and self-discipline, one can keep one's motives in check.

God looks at our motives in all we do. He determines who we are by our motives. One can do many good deeds in life while nurturing loving motives. Motives of cruelty and darkness, are that of sowing seeds of bitterness and emptiness . . . this serves only the master of destruction.

God blessed us with a gift of need. Our motives will determine how we fulfill that need. All are burdened with selfishness and at times motives of cruelty. God gave us a free will to decide which path we will take. One can resist the negative thoughts and needs or one can turn the negative to positive motives for the out-come of good for self and others.

We should use our motives, as a compass to guide us in life. No other increment of our being allows us to peer into one's deepest core, as our motives will. We should strive to make our hearts a sanctuary of motives that edify God's truths. In turn one will edify others and one's own life.

The Angel's Called Today

'tis I, the Angels came to sing songs of lullabies, comforting me with a cradling of assurance for absolute release. The Angels came to carry me high above my need of this earthly life. I surrendered to the sweetness of Serenity's peace. Freedom took my hand and I, gave flight to the call of Love's perfection . . . , I passed on, while you were unaware.

I gave my all to challenging triumphs and burdens be. I loved and lost and loved and gained . . . , not a moment in vain. I was strong in the good times and the bad, yet weakness bent my knees and there, I learned to be me.

Angels came to call today. I turned to listen to distant sounds of harmonious songs and awe, eternity's magnificence a cradling me with a brilliance of uplifting light and there, a choir of Angels stood in the midst of my room. I heard the call of all Glory in harmony. The sweetness of Wisdom's innocence called my will, with an all, surrendering bidding. All tales of the hereafter opened illuminated doors of peace and I surrendered to Angel's invitations songs. I turned in answer to God's hosts and there, my soul took a final, eternal flight.

In the realm of your pain, see me through the distance of tomorrow's endless light, for there is where my soul will forever rest. All my cares and beliefs became my truths . . . and now I am free.

My footsteps, my words never silent, for I will ever walk with you . . . I will ever be with you in loving memories. During this season of your sorrow, may the love we share, ever seek the light of our joy, which will always be. With Time's gifts of now and tomorrow, may my eternal presence and love for you, set you free.

Try Imagine

Try to imagine what God was thinking when He created you. Try to imagine and measure the love He was feeling at your conception in His thoughts. Try to imagine the pureness of His absolute love. Try to imagine this was His state when He made you to be. Try to imagine what He was thinking when He colored your hair, your eyes, your complexion . . . everything was chosen with His loving care. Try to imagine His special purpose for you, a single uniqueness so pure and true. Try to imagine His love and patience so great that He gave you a free will . . . with hopes, the loving instinct He embedded in your heart would never fade and keep you connected to Him, as earth's journey becomes quiet and still. Try to imagine a love so great, try to imagine with all you can feel, try to imagine with all your will . . . for God's love is so absolute and pure . . . so willing to endlessly endure. As much as we may try . . . a love so great we are yet to know . . . we can only try to imagine.

Calmness soothes the bite of anger.

What is Meekness to Me . . .

Meekness many times is misunderstood as weakness, yet when meekness is practiced as God intended, meekness is the opposite of weakness. Webster defines meekness as: showing patients and a gentle disposition, which is God's meaning of meekness. Webster goes on to define meekness as; lacking spirit or backbone; submissive. The latter, many times is the understanding that folks have of meekness. Many believe that being meek is a humiliating weakness.

Meekness, as God intends is a discipline that requires wisdom and a powerful strength. Meekness is a product of patience. Patience comes from time, wisdom and the practice of love for what is right. Meekness is a quiet obedience that brings one, so disciplined a peaceful heart.

Oft times when one displays meekness in any circumstance, the observers may consider one weak, unwilling to defend or protect one's self from an offense, yet meekness is a display of Godly strength. A strength that requires a power to recede one's self from oppositions . . . a wisdom to understand when meekness is best and the discipline to practice this enduring will.

Anyone can have a loose tongue. Think on this . . . how difficult is it to keep silence when we have been offended in any way by another? Many will not agree, yet most times, silence is golden. With an uninterested audience, the power of the unkind act, many times can be dissolved. The humbleness of a meek spirit can be a peace maker.

A meek spirit is a beautiful, disciplined spirit. Meekness exudes gentleness, kindness and understanding in times of opposition and joy. One who practices God's meekness is one who cherishes and loves peacefulness . . . one to express first thoughts of kindness . . . first acts of patience and understanding. This powerful strength of inner resolve and wisdom misunderstood by many . . . is meekness.

What is a True Friend . . .

Aside from one's love of God and family, one of our most valuable relationships in life is a true friend. Acquaintances come and go, yet some will not remember your name. The truth and love of a true friendship is everlasting.

The love between friends has a strength and an endurance that will not weaken or diminish in the worst of times. If one should stumble and/ or fall by the weight of life, the other is there to carry on for both without a plea or a questioning heart.

A true friend will not communicate with an analytic frame of mind. A true friend will accept us for who we are without expectations that are patterned by our world. A friend never searches for one's less than perfect qualities, for we all have flaws and faults. A true friend understands this. A true friend knows one's gifts and is the first to see the good within us.

When life is too much or not enough, a true friend will offer a timeless nurturing to help one to carry on. If all others doubt you, a true friend will know the truth that is within you. When one reaches one's finest hour, a true friend is never jealous, yet shares one's deepest joy. A friend will help one build, grow and lend us hope to become better and more, until we have achieved our best.

A true friend is a gift of love from God. A true friend is a blessing to one's self, to one's life.

What is Faith to Me . . .

When life's darkness is at my back, I lend my soul to quiet submission, as my heart knowingly searches His face . . . there I talk to Him and I know He can hear . . . He is listening to my words, the pleadings and joys of my heart . . . this is faith.

I look around me and see His mastery in all things of this great earth and I feel His love. I look to the stars, the lights of heaven and know He is there. I feel the warmth of the sun in Spring time, I feel the warm summer breeze at night, as I stand in the moon light, I feel love when I look into the face of a baby or feel the smile of an old folk . . . in all these things I feel Him so close . . . this is faith.

I listen to friends as they speak of their happiness, sadness, failures and hopes . . . I pray for them and know He will help. I answer the sharing of my friends with a genuine love . . . allowing a caring that is designed by God, for I want to be like Him . . . this is faith.

When I fail Him and do things against His plan for me . . . He tugs at my heart, then I turn around to find He is there to pull me up . . . to help me regain my forward journey. He understands that my efforts are honest and true, yet at times with a human blindness that leads me to an opposite place. My time of perfection is not of this life. I know when I loose my way, His gentle love is there to help me to regain my course . . . this is faith.

What is faith to me? Some say that faith is the most difficult will to practice and at times this is true, yet I think that many times we miss that our faith too, is in the simplest things. It is faith that allows us to see God's hand in all His wonderful gifts, which many times all of us take for granted. The recognition, inner knowledge and awareness of His presence in all things is faith. That feeling of love and warmth, as well, as the knowledge that we can go to Him and He awill help in times of trouble . . . just the seeking and acknowledgement of Him in anything . . . is faith.

Retaining bitterness is a power struggle between good and evil

You are His Signature

God is the Master Painter, Sculptor, Poet, and you are His signature. He created you with a passionate love beyond all earthly understanding. Focus on this truth with your entire being. Embrace your life, as the gift that it is. Cherish your qualities with an absolute awareness of your uniqueness. You are one and never to be duplicated. Is this not proof enough of your importance to God and His plan for your life, all life?

How few know that we are to love ourselves. Not as the world loves, for that is vanity. Vanity only manifests conceit. Vanity has no real worth, no real depth. Vanity is merely a false pretense of God's true love. Vanity is a mask that covers God's truth. Vanity is a corrupt thief that can steal away God's purposes of true love for one's self.

The love that I speak of is the love that comes from knowledge that your life is a gift. Your journey in this life is the unwrapping of that gift and maturing to a place of awareness and appreciation, with awe the spirit of you . . . a place to learn God's purposes for you . . . loving yourself brings understanding of God's true love for you.

I try to focus on the positives of life, therefore I am speaking to you about your goodness and reason for being. What joy and peace one can know with the loving acceptance of self. With the realization of one's self-worth, one can grow, become and be what God intended.

God is the Master Painter, Sculptor, Poet and you are His signature, He created all things with perfection and you are a part of His perfect Masterpiece.

Your Reflection

Look in the mirror, what do you see? The image that you see should be a beautiful person looking back at you. God molded every angle, color and contour of what you see. He made everything about you so unique and beautiful.

Many times we compare ourselves to a "movie star" image. It will not be possible for most of us to achieve this reflection. This is not a God creation, yet a creation man made to achieve monetary gain. Look past that to you. Look at you . . . the most precious creation that God manifested from His absolute love. You were designed by God. How awesome is that!! Please pause and think on this. Please pause and think on this when you entertain negative thoughts allowing a blindness of your true beauty.

There should be no argument on this. If there is, then you are relying on your old self image, for if it is negative, then it is an untrue image of you. We all have uniquely different appearances. This is the beauty of our own uniqueness. This is a gift from God.

Many times when we look at our reflection, we are seeing the negative remarks and/or opinions of others. This may be allowing you to over-ride the true reflection in the mirror. Why allow the insecurity of another to steal your image of true beauty? Most times that selfish person cannot see his/her own beautiful reflection and has a need to bring another to their self made lowly place.

Look in the mirror, what do you see? If you do not see a beautiful person looking back at you, then you are only seeing a reflection of a negative image projected from yourself made opinion. You are seeing a false image . . . not the true and beautiful reflection God created, . . . for you truly are beautiful.

The Lord did not put limits and expiration dates on anything in the pursuit of good.

The author wrote this book to allow the reader to consider a more positive way of seeing others and every life situation. Each writing and poem is meant to have a positive outcome for everyone.